Ralph Waldo Emerson

Proceedings at the Centennial Celebration of Concord Fight, April 19, 1875

Ralph Waldo Emerson

Proceedings at the Centennial Celebration of Concord Fight, April 19, 1875

ISBN/EAN: 9783744747202

Printed in Europe, USA, Canada, Australia, Japan

Cover: Foto ©ninafisch / pixelio.de

More available books at **www.hansebooks.com**

PROCEEDINGS

AT THE

CENTENNIAL CELEBRATION

OF

CONCORD FIGHT

April 19, 1875.

CONCORD, MASS.
PUBLISHED BY THE TOWN.
1876.

PREFACE.

The committee chosen by the town of Concord at the March meeting, 1874, and clothed with full powers to prepare for and carry out a centennial celebration of Concord Fight, deeming the occasion worthy of a more complete and permanent record than could be obtained in the columns of the newspapers, and wishing to furnish to those who were attracted to Concord by the national importance of the first Centennial of the American Revolution, and by the patriotic memories it awakened, an opportunity of preserving in a permanent form an official history of our ceremonies, and feeling it to be their duty also to render to the town an account of the manner in which they executed their trust, delegated to the undersigned the task of preparing and publishing such an account, which is herewith respectfully submitted as the Report of the Committee of Arrangements. Their financial statement appears in the Town Report for 1875-6.

The Nineteenth of April, 1775, has always been regarded by the people of New England as the national birthday; and its fiftieth and seventy-fifth anniversaries were celebrated at Concord by the towns of Middlesex, Essex, and Norfolk, whose men shared with the men of our town the dangers and glories of that day.

But the people of Concord believed that the hundredth anniversary of the opening of the Revolutionary War would be recognized universally as of national interest, and that their preparations for the celebration of it should be on a scale commensurate with the importance of the occasion.

We have thought it best, in writing this report, to adhere to the chronological order of events; and therefore — as the preparation for the Centennial began with the project of a monument to be placed where Davis and Hosmer fell, and Buttrick gave the first order to fire on the king's troops — we have begun with a brief account of the Minute-man and its origin.

The religious services on the morning of Sunday, April 18, were held in the Old Meeting House, where the first Provincial Congress assembled. As these services were memorial in their character, and were attended by the President and his Cabinet, and by many other honored guests of the town, it may properly be said that the commemoration began on that day.

Although the ball was not a part of the celebration for which the Committee considered themselves authorized to expend the money of the town, yet any account of our proceedings would be sadly incomplete, that should omit all mention of that brilliant and beautiful scene. We have, therefore, concluded our report with a short account of the ball.

Appended hereto is a carefully prepared abstract of the literature of the Nineteenth of April, kindly furnished at our request by our townsman, James L. Whitney, the assistant superintendent of the Boston Public Library; including a heliotype facsimile of the famous Diary of Rev. William Emerson.

We have used our best endeavors to make this chronicle of a day so dear to us a complete and true one. Yet we are conscious that there was much in our celebration — the proud and tender memories, the sympathy, the spirit, the thanksgiving that moved the hearts of our people — of too fine and evanescent a quality for any record, however vivid or faithful, adequately to convey.

SAMUEL HOAR,
EDWARD W. EMERSON, } *for the Committee.*
CHARLES H. WALCOTT,

TABLE OF CONTENTS.

		PAGES.
I.	THE MINUTE-MAN AND THE BRIDGE	11–17
II.	THE PREPARATIONS	21–44
III.	SUNDAY SERVICES	47–60
IV.	THE PROCESSION	63–74
V.	EXERCISES IN THE ORATION TENT	77–119
VI.	EXERCISES IN THE DINNER TENT	123–156
VII.	THE BALL	159

THE NINETEENTH OF APRIL IN LITERATURE	165
APPENDIX	175

THE MINUTE-MAN AND THE BRIDGE.

THE MINUTE-MAN AND THE BRIDGE.

To the People of Concord:

It is fit that a public record of Concord's Centennial Celebration of the Fight at the North Bridge should recognize how that celebration was inspired and moulded by the thought of one man, an old citizen, who himself passed away without the sight of that fulfilment of his desire in which his townsmen take such pride to-day.

A picture still fresh in the memory of almost every inhabitant of Concord is the bowed form and wrinkled face of EBENEZER HUBBARD.

Living in the house where he boasted that his grandfather entertained Hancock and the patriots of the Continental Congress which met in the old meeting-house, tilling the old flat fields, or walking in the stately woods, which he kept almost sacred from the axe,—he remembered with pride the Middlesex farmers, who took the dread responsibility of attacking the troops of Great Britain.

The old North Bridge, whose planks had been trodden by those men, was taken down when he was ten years old; and it grieved him that it should be only a tradition to the younger generations of Concord, and that no stone should mark the spot where Buttrick gave the word to fire.

At the state muster, in 1869, Mr. Hubbard walked to the camp, and made his way to headquarters, to try to interest Gen. Butler in his favorite scheme; for his hope was to rouse, in some way, the attention of Congress to the importance of the renewal of the bridge, and the fitly marking the spot where the first patriot volley was fired. He failed entirely in this interview, but went home, probably the more resolved to do his part. The following year, one October morning, the neighbors found him sitting in his chair, dead.

He made by his will a bequest to the town in these words:—

"I order my executor to pay the sum of one thousand dollars towards building a monument in said town of Concord, on the spot where the Americans fell, on the opposite side of the river from the present monument, in the battle of the 19th of April, 1775, providing my said executor shall ascertain that said monument first named has been built, or sufficient funds have been obtained therefor, within five years after my decease; but in case my executor shall have ascertained that said first-named monument is not built, nor sufficient funds obtained for that purpose, within five years after my decease, then I order my executor to pay over to Hancock, N.H., said sum of one thousand dollars."

Mr. Hubbard further placed in the hands of the town treasurer the sum of six hundred dollars, towards the expense of building a bridge over the river, on the site of the old one.

Stedman Buttrick, grandson of Major John Buttrick who commanded the American force at the bridge, gave a deed to the town of about one-quarter of an acre of land, in his meadow on the west bank of the river, "at the butment of the old North Bridge," "for the purpose of erecting a Monument there, and for no other purpose, and on condition that the grantee shall make and forever maintain a fence around the same, and that a bridge shall be constructed across the river, from the easterly side, to pass to the above premises, and without any right of way over my land."

Mr. Buttrick also died (November, 1874) without seeing the completion of the work that his patriotic gift had aided.

At the March meeting, 1872, a committee was chosen, to consider what action should be taken by the town in relation to the bequest of Ebenezer Hubbard. It consisted of the following gentlemen: John S. Keyes, Chairman; George Heywood, George M. Brooks, John B. Moore, and Addison G. Fay.

At the meeting in March, 1873, this committee reported the terms of the bequest of Mr. Hubbard, and the gift of Mr. Buttrick, and recommended that the town should gratefully accept the patriotic bequest and gift of its citizens, and that it should "procure a statue of a Continental Minute-man, cut in granite, and erect it on a proper foundation, on the American side of the river," with the opening stanza of the poem by Ralph Waldo Emerson, sung at the dedication of the Battle Monument in 1837, "enduringly engraven for an inscription on the base;" also "that a suitable bridge be constructed to give access to the spot;" and, finally, "that the work be completed and dedicated on the one hundredth anniversary of the day, with such other exercises as may be hereafter determined."

A vote of the town was passed at the same meeting, authorizing the same committee to procure designs and estimates for a statue. Mr. Fay having died, Mr. Henry F. Smith was appointed on the committee in his place.

At the November meeting, 1873, a small plaster model of a minute-man, executed by Mr. Daniel C. French of Concord, was submitted by the committee, and the town voted to accept the design, and appropriated the sum of five hundred dollars towards the expense of procuring a full-sized model to be made by him, the artist generously leaving all question of compensation for his design, other than the mere expense of construction, to the free will of the town.

Five persons, Messrs. R. W. Emerson, Frederic Hudson, George A. King, Andrew J. Harlow, and William W. Wilde, were added to the committee, which, thus enlarged, was authorized to decide on the material for the statue, to procure a suitable base and carry on the work.

Early in the year 1874, the General Court passed the following act, entitled, "An Act authorizing the Town of Concord to raise Money for a Monument and for its Dedication."

Be it enacted, &c.

SECTION 1. — The Town of Concord is authorized to raise by taxation, such sums of money as may be needed for a suitable monument at the "Old North Bridge," to commemorate the events of the nineteenth day of April, seventeen hundred and seventy-five, and for an appropriate celebration at its dedication.

SECT. 2. — This Act shall take effect upon its passage.

Approved March 9, 1874.

In the March meeting, 1874, the town appropriated the sum of fifteen hundred dollars, to be used in procuring a suitable base to the statue and completing the work. A committee of thirty citizens was chosen at the same meeting to make arrangements for a fitting Centennial Celebration of Concord Fight.

The original plan for a granite statue was abandoned by the Monument Committee, and bronze was selected as the material best adapted to Mr. French's design, and most enduring in our climate.

Through the influence and energetic action of the Hon. E. R. Hoar, our Representative in the Forty-third Congress, the following act[2] passed the House of Representatives on April 18, and the Senate, April 20 (the 19th being Sunday), and was approved by the President, April 22.

---

[1] Statute 1874, c. 49.

[2] A beautifully illuminated copy of this act, attested by the Secretary of State, was presented by him to Judge Hoar, and given to the Free Public Library by the latter gentleman.

Be it enacted by the Senate and House of Representatives of the United States of America, in Congress assembled,

That the Secretary of War be, and is hereby, authorized to deliver to the municipal authorities of Concord, Massachusetts, ten pieces of condemned brass cannon, to be used in the erection of a monument at the Old North Bridge, to commemorate the first repulse of the troops of Great Britain in the war of the Revolution, on the nineteenth day of April, seventeen hundred and seventy-five.

J. G. BLAINE,
Speaker of the House of Representatives.

M. H. CARPENTER,
President of Senate pro tempore.

Approved April 22, 1874.
U. S. GRANT.

The cannon were sent soon after to the Ames Manufacturing Company at Chicopee, Mass., and the model early in the autumn.

The committee decided to reproduce, in its essential features, the old battle bridge, though on a lighter scale, and was fortunately enabled to do this by the rude old wood engraving of Concord Fight, made with that faithfulness of detail which characterizes most untutored art, by Earl and Doolittle, two members of Benedict Arnold's Horse Guards, who rode up from the camp at Cambridge one July day in 1775 and made the sketch on the spot, supplying the attacking farmers and retreating red-coats to the picture from the stories told them by the sharers in the fight. This picture showed a plain wooden bridge spanning the river, with a slight arch, supported by a few rows of piles.

Mr. Reuben N. Rice generously undertook to add some decoration to the rigid simplicity of the old model, and obtained a plan from Mr. William R. Emerson of Boston, in which the place of the rough railing of "followers" of the old bridge was supplied by a paling of graceful pattern, made of cedars with the bark on; and two rustic half-arbors were placed on the middle of the bridge, projecting over the water, with seats where pilgrims might sit and watch the quiet river brimming its meadows. The bridge was built during the summer and autumn according to this plan.

But how to place the Minute-man to best advantage when he came? Many forms of pedestal were suggested, simple and elaborate. The plan which pleased the committee more than any other, was to haul to the spot one of the great boulders that are found in Concord fields, and thus set the bronze farmer on a pedestal of some old glacier's carving, merely smoothing a place on the front to receive the inscription. The practical difficulties of this scheme were found insurmountable.

In the oak woods on the edge of the neighboring town of Westford (whence, on the battle morning, came that Lieutenant-Colonel John Robinson, who marched, at Major Buttrick's request, by his side down the hill to the attack), lay a rock of fine white granite, out of which, thirty-nine years ago, came the old battle monument. From this a great block was split by Mr. John Cole of that town, so nearly rectangular and perfect that it almost tempted the Monument Committee to place it under the statue without further work upon it. This was brought to Concord when the snow fell. Finally a plan, kindly furnished the Committee by Mr. J. Elliot Cabot of Brookline, by which they could use this stone, was adopted, and the work executed by Mr. Cole during the winter.

The body of the pedestal is one block seven feet high, with equal faces four feet broad, the front face rough pointed, but having a sunk panel, fine hammered, across the middle of which, in incised and bronzed letters, are these lines of Emerson: —

> BY THE RUDE BRIDGE THAT ARCHED THE FLOOD
> THEIR FLAG TO APRIL'S BREEZE UNFURLED,
> HERE ONCE THE EMBATTLED FARMERS STOOD
> AND FIRED THE SHOT HEARD ROUND THE WORLD.

The rear face is similar to the front, and on the panel in high relief the inscription: —

· 1775

NINETEENTH

OF

APRIL

◢◣

1875

The lateral faces of the pedestal are rough hewn, with a smooth hammered margin six inches and a half wide. This main block is supported by a base projecting six inches and a half, and nine inches high, resting on a turfed mound three feet high.

The whole lot given by Mr. Buttrick has been filled, so as to raise it to the level of the old abutment, and above the spring floods of the river, and its edges turfed, while a sufficiently broad gravel drive passes round the monument. A willow hedge has been planted round the grounds, to further protect the abutment from the floods. Where the statue stands, a deep pit was dug and filled with rubble for a firmer foundation.

The site itself is in the line of the middle of the bridge, and one hundred and ten feet from its western end, in front of the old sprouting apple-stump, that tradition says was the spot where Captain Isaac Davis received his death-wound, — "the burning bush where God spake for His people."

In March the pedestal was set in place, and under it a hermetically sealed copper box containing —

    The History of the Monument, by the Chairman of the Monument Committee.
    A copy of Shattuck's History of Concord.
    The account of the Fight, from the Diary of Rev. William Emerson.
    A Pamphlet, giving an account of the Celebration in 1850.
    A Pamphlet, giving an account of the Dedication of the Soldier's Monument in the Square, April 19, 1867.
    The Town Report for 1874.
    Photographs of the Artist and of the Statue.
    Map of the Village in 1775.
    Map of Concord, 1855.
    Map of the Centre of the Town in 1874.
    Coins, Stamps, Newspapers of the Day, Invitations to the Celebration, &c.

During the first days of April, the statue, which had been most successfully cast from the gun-metal, arrived from Chicopee, and was set upon the pedestal, and after a few days was veiled to await the formal uncovering on the anniversary of the battle.

It represents a young farmer, one of the minute-men of that day, leaving his plough in the furrow on the alarm of the approach of the regulars, and answering, musket in hand, the call to arms; one of those,

> "Whose faith and truth
> On war's red touchstone rang true metal;
> Who ventured life and love and youth
> For the great prize of death in battle."

There is nothing hot or theatrical in the movement, which is considered, and the face serious, as of one who sees all the doubt and danger from the first and yet goes quietly on.

The figure is of heroic proportions, being seven feet high, yet has the lightness of a man skilled in wood-craft as well as farm labor. The anatomy and poise are conscientiously studied from nature; and even the long waistcoat, hanging heavy with the bullets in its pockets, the worn gaiters and rude accoutrements show faithful work and historical accuracy. It has been noticed that the statue wins praise alike from the scholar and the laborer, the cultivated and the untrained taste.

Mr. French is only twenty-five years old, and this is his first work of importance. The town cannot fail to be long grateful to him for the good work he has done, and the charm he has added to its meadows.

THE PREPARATIONS.

THE PREPARATIONS.

AFTER the appointment of the Monument Committee and the acceptance of the model presented with their first report at the March meeting in 1873, the next step taken by the town, in its municipal capacity, was to appoint a Committee of Arrangements, whose duty it was to prepare a suitable celebration at the dedication of the statue, on the 19th of April, 1875.

The necessary authority to raise money for the purpose by taxation had been conferred by the Legislature; and at the annual town meeting held March 30, 1874, it was voted,

"That a committee of thirty be chosen as a Committee of Arrangements for the celebration of the Centennial Anniversary of Concord Fight, and that the Committee be authorized to expend a sum not exceeding five thousand dollars for the purpose."

Such a committee was then chosen, consisting of the following persons; viz., —

GEORGE KEYES, SAMUEL HOAR, FREDERIC HUDSON,
EDWARD C. DAMON, REUBEN N. RICE,
ALFRED B. C. DAKIN,

JOSEPH D. BROWN, RICHARD F. BARRETT, ELIJAH WOOD,
SAMUEL W. BROWN, HUMPHREY H. BUTTRICK,
JAMES C. MELVIN,

LEVI MILES, WILLIAM BUTTRICK, WILLIAM F. HURD,
SIDNEY J. BARRETT, EDWIN WHEELER,
HENRY L. SHATTUCK,

JAMES D. WRIGHT, LEWIS FLINT, JOSEPH DERBY, JUN.,
WILLIAM H. HUNT, EDWARD W. EMERSON,
HENRY J. WALCOTT,

CHARLES THOMPSON, ALBERT E. WOOD, ANDREW J. HARLOW,
CHARLES D. TUTTLE, MARCELLUS HOUGHTON,
SYLVESTER LOVEJOY.

Messrs. Hudson, **Rice, Miles,** and Hurd having **declined to** serve, the vacancies thus **occasioned were** filled by the **committee, subject to the ratification of the town,** by the election of

RICHARD BARRETT, GEORGE P. HOW, CHARLES H. WALCOTT, JAMES B. WOOD.

This **action was approved and ratified by the town** at the following March meeting.[1]

The Committee of Arrangements held its first meeting at the Town Hall on Thursday, June 25, and organized with the choice of the following officers: George Keyes, *Chairman;* Samuel Hoar, *Secretary;* and Henry J. Walcott, *Treasurer.* Subsequently, the following sub-committees were chosen by the committee of thirty; viz., —

On General Invitations.
E. R. HOAR, R. W. EMERSON, GEORGE HEYWOOD.

On the Oration.
CHARLES H. WALCOTT, EDWARD C. DAMON, SAMUEL HOAR.

On the Dinner.
JOSEPH D. BROWN, CHARLES THOMPSON, EDWARD W. EMERSON, JAMES C. MELVIN, CHARLES H. WALCOTT.

To invite Participating Towns.
GEORGE KEYES, WILLIAM H. HUNT, JOSEPH D. BROWN, E. C. DAMON, H. J. WALCOTT, CHARLES THOMPSON, HENRY L. SHATTUCK.

On Music.
SAMUEL W. BROWN, A. J. HARLOW, R. F. BARRETT.

---

[1] At the annual town meeting, held March 29, 1875, the following votes were passed: —

"*Voted,* That the action of the Committee of Arrangements for the Centennial **Celebration of Concord Fight,** in filling vacancies in their number, be approved and ratified.

"*Voted,* That the Committee of Arrangements be authorized to expend **a sum not exceeding five thousand dollars, in addition to** the sums already authorized.

"*Voted,* That the sum of five thousand dollars be raised by taxation to defray the expenses of the Centennial Celebration, and that the treasurer be authorized to borrow such **further sum, not exceeding fifty-five** hundred dollars, as may be needed for that purpose."

On the Press.
W. W. WHEILDON, F. B. SANBORN, FREDERIC HUDSON, GEORGE TOLMAN.

On Military.
RICHARD BARRETT, GEORGE P. HOW, A. B. C. DAKIN, EDWIN WHEELER, JOSEPH DERBY, Jun.

On Decorations.
JAMES C. MELVIN, H. L. SHATTUCK, E. W. EMERSON, A. E. WOOD, WILLIAM BUTTRICK, LEWIS FLINT, CHARLES THOMPSON, SYLVESTER LOVEJOY.

On the Ball.
H. J. WALCOTT, H. H. BUTTRICK, R. F. BARRETT, S. J. BARRETT, J. D. WRIGHT, S. W. BROWN, SAMUEL HOAR, C. D. TUTTLE, J. D. BROWN, GEORGE P. HOW, JAMES B. WOOD.

On Transportation.
GEORGE KEYES, A. J. HARLOW, ELIJAH WOOD, J. D. BROWN, E. C. DAMON, M. HOUGHTON.

On Reception of Guests.
GEORGE M. BROOKS, R. W. EMERSON, GEORGE HEYWOOD, FREDERIC HUDSON, H. F. SMITH, JOHN S. KEYES, STEDMAN BUTTRICK, JOHN B. MOORE, W. W. WILDE, GEORGE A. KING.

Executive Committee.
GEORGE KEYES, RICHARD BARRETT, SAMUEL HOAR, CHARLES H. WALCOTT, JAMES C. MELVIN.

The four committees first chosen were called "joint committees to act with similar committees from Lexington;" but at a meeting of the Committee of Arrangements, October 17, 1874, a joint celebration having proved to be impracticable, their character was changed to that of "committees empowered to act in the Concord celebration for the purposes for which they were chosen."

The first proposition for a joint celebration of the events of the 19th of April, 1775, by the towns of Concord and Lexington, was made in a letter from a committee chosen by the latter town, addressed to the selectmen of Concord, and dated November 12, 1873.[1] This communication solicited the good services of our selectmen in awakening an interest among the people of our town; so that, before any specific arrangements were made, we might be enabled to participate with them in preparing for a union celebration at Lexington.

Our selectmen sent a reply, saying, in effect, that our town had already chosen a committee, eight months before the receipt of the letter from Lexington, to procure a model for a statue of a minuteman of '75, to be dedicated on the centennial anniversary; that the committee had reported at the last town meeting, which took place before the letter was received from Lexington; and that the work on the statue was already under way.[2]

This previous action of our town rendered any other action by the selectmen impossible without further proceedings in town meeting; and no further propositions were made looking to a union celebration at Lexington, previous events having made it certain that the people of Concord desired and expected to have in their own town a celebration which should appropriately commemorate the deeds of the men whom they delight to honor.

As soon as it clearly appeared that each of the towns had planned a celebration for itself, it was conceived that it might be practicable to agree upon such a division of the day, with a programme to be carried out in both towns, as should bring about a union celebration of a day and events in which they were jointly interested. But, after much negotiation, it was found that no satisfactory arrangement of time could be agreed upon and carried out; and, therefore, the idea was abandoned.

However much this result may have been regretted at the time, the event proved how disastrous would have been any attempt to carry out one programme including exercises in both towns.

From and after October 17, 1874, the single purpose of this Committee was to prepare a celebration which should be in accordance with the ideas of the people of Concord and in keeping with the magnitude of the occasion and the high official position of the guests who were expected to be present. The several sub-committees met frequently, and regularly reported progress to the general committee. The work was continually growing under their hands, as the people of the state

[1] See Appendix, A.   [2] See Appendix, B.

and nation came more and more to realize the importance of the approaching anniversary.

Special invitations were sent to the President and Vice-President of the United States, and members of the Cabinet, the United States Senators and Representatives from New England, the Judges of the Supreme Court of the United States, the Governors of the thirteen original states of the Union and their subdivisions, the Council and Legislature and Judiciary of Massachusetts, the President and Fellows and the Faculty of Harvard University, the Society of the Cincinnati, the Ancient and Honorable Artillery Company, the Bunker Hill Monument Association, the Massachusetts Historical Society, the New England Historic-Genealogical Society, the American Antiquarian Society, and many distinguished individuals.

It was planned that the governor of each New England state should appear in the procession escorted by the representative military organization of his state, as follows: The Governor of Massachusetts by the Newburyport Veteran Artillery Association, of Newburyport;[1] the Governor of Maine by the Portland Mechanic Blues, of Portland; the Governor of New Hampshire by the Amoskeag Veterans, of Manchester; the Governor of Vermont by the Ransom Guards, of St. Albans; the Governor of Rhode Island by the First Light Infantry Veteran Association, of Providence; the Governor of Connecticut by the Putnam Phalanx, of Hartford.

General invitations were extended to the inhabitants of the towns and cities that furnished men who actually bore arms in Concord on the 19th of April, 1775, or whose men participated in the events of the day elsewhere.

Those of the first-named class were Acton, Bedford, Billerica, Carlisle, Chelmsford, Lincoln, Littleton, Stow, Sudbury, and Westford.

The second and larger class consisted of Arlington, Belmont, Beverly, Boston [Charlestown and Roxbury], Boxborough, Brookline, Burlington, Cambridge, Danvers, Dedham, Everett, Framingham, Lexington, Lowell, Lynn, Lynnfield, Maynard, Medford, Melrose, Needham, Newton, Norwood, Peabody, Pepperell, Reading, Salem, Somerville, Topsfield, Wakefield, Waltham, Watertown, Wayland, Weston, Winchester, and Woburn.[2]

---

[1] In point of fact, the Newburyport Veterans acted as escort to the Legislature of Massachusetts, the Independent Corps of Cadets having been ordered out to serve as escort to the Governor and Council.

[2] Probably the towns of Marlborough and Stoneham should have been included; but their claims were not called to the attention of the committee until after the celebration.

In addition to the invitations which were intended to include all the citizens of the towns named, a card was also sent to the town clerk of each of those towns, inviting a delegation, consisting of the town officers and settled clergymen, to attend as the guests of the town of Concord. In the cities, this latter invitation was to the mayor and aldermen or to the mayor and a committee of the city government.

The form of invitation to the guests of the town was engraved on steel, was adorned by a heliotype of the "Minute-man,"[1] and read as follows: —

1775.   CONCORD FIGHT.   1875.

April 19th, 1775.

To

Sir, — *The Inhabitants of the town of Concord, Massachusetts, cordially invite to be present as their guest at Concord, on the Nineteenth of April, 1875, and to join with them in celebrating the centennial anniversary of the opening of the Revolutionary War.*

E. R. HOAR,
R. W. EMERSON, } *Committee*
GEORGE HEYWOOD, } *of Invitation.*

Knowledge of our approaching festival was still more widely spread by a notice, which was prepared and signed by the whole Committee of Arrangements, and was as follows: —

1775.   *CONCORD FIGHT.*   1875.

DEAR SIR:

The town of Concord, Massachusetts, purposes to celebrate the Centennial Anniversary of Concord Fight on the Nineteenth of April, 1875, in a manner appropriate to the importance of that day which " made conciliation impossible and independence certain." The exercises will consist of an oration by George William Curtis, Esq., of New York; a grand military and civic procession to the site of the "Old North Bridge;" the unveiling and dedication of a bronze statue of a Minute-Man on the spot where Davis and

---

[1] This heliotype, taken from the clay model before casting, precedes this part of our report.

Hosmer fell, and where was "fired the shot heard round the world;" a public dinner, with toasts and speeches, and a grand ball in the evening.

The President of the United States and his Cabinet; the Governor, Legislature and Judiciary of Massachusetts; the Governors of each of the New England States, and many other distinguished men are expected to be present as the guests of the town.

The people of Acton, Bedford, Beverly, Billerica, Brookline, Cambridge, Charlestown, Chelmsford, Danvers, Dedham, Framingham, Lexington, Lynn, Medford, Needham, Newton, Roxbury, Salem, Stow, Sudbury, Watertown, and Woburn, have been invited to participate in the celebration, as their fathers did in the struggle for liberty.

The town of Concord hopes that all those who are connected with her by descent or affection will join with her in this interesting commemoration.

Very truly yours,

CONCORD, MASS., *January*, 1875.

This was printed in most of the New York and New England papers, and was sent by mail in all directions. The object of this publication was to inform the descendants of Concord people, scattered all over the country, of the preparations that were being made, and of the desire of our citizens that all who loved the old town should be present on this memorable occasion. This notice was widely circulated, and, so far as your committee are able to judge, had the desired effect.

From the beginning your Committee felt that it was the earnest desire of every citizen of Concord that the town of Acton, with its glorious memories of the day we were about to celebrate, should be considered as a guest entitled to peculiar honor. Accordingly, in addition to the invitations already described, which were sent to other towns as well, a special invitation was extended to the people of Acton and their company of minute-men. The Executive Committee also sent the following letter, which was read at a special town meeting in Acton : —

CONCORD, Jan. 9, 1875.

TO THE SELECTMEN OF ACTON.

Gentlemen, — The Committee of Arrangements for the Centennial Celebration of Concord Fight, chosen by the town of Concord, desire the co-operation of the town of Acton in the approaching celebration, April 19, 1875.

Formal invitations have been sent to all the towns whose men participated in the first armed struggle for liberty, to join with Concord in the proper celebration of the day, and you have undoubtedly received yours; but it seems to this committee, and it is the desire of the town of Concord, that the town of Acton should receive something more than a formal invitation.

Davis and Hosmer, men of Acton, were the first martyrs to organized resistance to the British crown; and on the spot where they fell it is proposed to erect an emblematical statue of a minute-man, and to dedicate it with appropriate ceremonies. At its dedication the citizens of Acton should have a prominent part

As Acton joined with Concord in that famous fight; as Acton joined with Concord in 1825, and again in 1850, in celebrating their common anniversary; as Concord joined with Acton at the dedication of your monument in 1851,— so we hope that Acton will now join with Concord, and make a commemoration that shall of itself be memorable.

We trust, therefore, that you, or some committee on the part of your town, will confer with us as soon as practicable with reference to the arrangements for the forthcoming celebration.

We are, gentlemen, very respectfully, your obedient servants,

<blockquote>
GEORGE KEYES,
RICHARD BARRETT,
SAMUEL HOAR,
CHARLES H. WALCOTT,
JAMES C. MELVIN,
</blockquote>

For the Concord Committee of Arrangements.

At the same meeting, the people of Acton accepted our invitation and passed the following resolution:—

Whereas, The nineteenth day of April next will be the one hundredth anniversary of Concord Fight and the Battle of Lexington, in the former of which engagements the men of Acton had an active and most honorable part, Capt. Isaac Davis and private Abner Hosmer falling in the former engagement, and private James Hayward at Lexington on the retreat, we, the citizens of Acton, in town meeting assembled, deem it due to the memory of our patriotic dead, and to our own sense of obligation to them for what they did for us, to celebrate the day, as a town, in some appropriate manner; and

Whereas, The towns of Concord and Lexington have both, through their committees, cordially invited us to join them in celebrating the day in their respective towns, a courtesy that we fully recognize; yet, inasmuch as it was at Concord that the Acton company was more especially engaged and distinguished, and as a part of the celebration of the day in Concord is to consist in the dedication of a monument to be erected upon the spot where Davis and Hosmer fell, an act of justice to them and their co-patriots which we greatly appreciate: therefore

Resolved, That, while we would have gladly coöperated with both of those towns in the observance of the day, we feel it our more especial duty, and we do hereby cordially accept the invitation of the town of Concord, to join them in celebrating the coming 19th of April, 1875; and

Voted, That a committee of ten be chosen to confer with the town of Concord through their committee, in reference to said celebration, and that said committee have power and be instructed in behalf of the town of Acton to make all necessary arrangements for the proper celebration of that day.

In the spirit of the above resolution, the Acton people attended in large numbers, and with a fine looking body of minute-men dressed in uniform.

In issuing invitations, whether to the national and state officials, to towns, associations, or individuals, it was borne in mind that our anniversary would not only have strong attractions for the people of Concord and of Massachusetts, but would be national. It is hardly an exaggeration to say that the people of the entire country viewed with deep interest the preparations which were being made by our town properly to commemorate the centennial recurrence of the day on which the nation was born, and to the issues of which we all owe so much of our happiness and prosperity as free American citizens.

At an early day, the President of the United States and several members of his Cabinet expressed their interest in the preparations, and their desire and intention to be present in Concord on the 19th.

The following passage occurs in the Inaugural Address of Gov. Gaston to the Legislature:—

"I take pleasure in communicating to you an invitation from the inhabitants of the town of Concord to the two branches of the General Court, to be present as the guests of the town on the 19th of April next, and take part in a fitting commemoration of the events which make the day famous. A similar invitation from Concord was accepted by your predecessors twenty-five years ago; and I commend this invitation to your favorable consideration."

Subsequently our invitation was accepted by both branches of the General Court, and a joint special committee[1] was appointed to confer with the Governor as to the arrangements for the attendance of the Legislature.

An order was adopted April 5, authorizing this committee of the Legislature to extend the hospitalities of the state to the President, Vice-President, and members of the Cabinet; and to make all such

---

[1] This committee consisted of Messrs. Joseph A. Harwood of Littleton, and Francis E. Ison of Hadley, on the part of the Senate; and Moses Williams, jun., of Brookline, William E. Blunt of Haverhill, Dexter A. Tompkins of Boston, Thomas F. Fitzgerald of Boston, and Isaac T. Burr of Newton, on the part of the House of Representatives.

arrangements as they might deem necessary and **proper for the purpose of receiving and** providing for their guests.

After conferring with the President, and with the Governor and Council, the programme **agreed upon** by the joint special committee was as follows : —

"That the Legislature, together with the Governor and Council, **and invited guests of the Commonwealth,** proceed to Concord on Monday the 19th of April, for the purpose of joining there the President of the United States, and with him attending the centennial exercises at Concord, until the hour of one o'clock, P.M. ; and that, at that hour, the Legislature, and Governor and Council, with the guests of the Commonwealth, proceed promptly to Lexington, for the purpose of attending the centennial exercises of that town during the remainder of the day."[1] This order of proceedings was determined upon, April 6, and was adhered to as strictly as the crowds and the irregularity of trains would allow. The President and his Cabinet had previously accepted an invitation to come to Concord on the night of Saturday the 17th, and become the guests of Judge Hoar until Monday morning, after which time they would be the guests of the town during the forenoon, and again in the evening.[2]

In view of the fact that our celebration was to be a national one, an enormous quantity of flags and uncut bunting was despatched to Concord from the navy yards at Portsmouth, Boston, New York, and Washington, to be used by the committee in decorating the streets, tents, and buildings in the town. The Secretary of the Navy detailed Lieut. Commander Henry H. Gorringe with orders to take charge of the flags, and render any assistance in his power.

It is due the department, as well as to Lieut. Commander Gorringe, to say that the Committee feel under the greatest obligations to both. We cannot be too grateful for this generous loan of decorating material, or praise too highly the efficient manner in which the directions of the Secretary were carried out by the officer in charge.[3]

[1] Report of committee given to the press, April 7, and signed by Messrs. Harwood and Williams.

[2] It was one of the unfortunate occurrences of the day, that, on account of the great crowds, and the unavoidable delay occasioned by them, the President was not met at Lexington by the carriage which was sent for him from Concord at his request ; his plan having been to return to Concord, and attend the ball in the evening.

[3] Exclusive of rags and scraps of bunting that were not used, and not counting any of the flags and bunting from the Boston yard, we had the use of 6,769 flags belonging to the Government, the invoice price of which, as appears by the official records, was $38,704.57. The Boston yard supplied a large additional number of flags, and a large quantity of uncut bunting.

THE PREPARATIONS.

The Agricultural Hall, the tents for the oration and dinner, the public buildings, the liberty-pole, and the principal streets, were decorated under the direction of the sub-committee chosen for the purpose. They employed Messrs. Lamprell and Marble, of Boston, to see that the work was properly done; and the results attained by the decorators were perfectly satisfactory to the Committee, and, it is believed, to the people of the town.

Many private buildings were appropriately decorated; but, as they did not come properly within the province of the committee, it is not attempted, in this place, to give a description of the beautiful masses and combinations of color that made the whole town resplendent on this gala day.

At the request of the Committee of Arrangements the Marine Band of Washington was ordered to Concord to take part in our procession, on the sole condition that the town should entertain its members while they remained in Concord, without expense to the department. It was considered very fitting that the highest officials of the nation should be accompanied in the procession by this celebrated band of musicians, regularly enlisted into the service of the United States, with our own Concord Artillery as military escort. The band also rendered valuable assistance at the promenade concert in the evening.

At a meeting held November 7, 1874, the Executive Committee was instructed to report at the next meeting " a programme for the whole celebration of the hundredth anniversary of Concord Fight."

After mature deliberation, it was finally settled that the day should begin with the formation of the procession, in the immediate neighborhood of the Fitchburg Railroad station ; that the procession should march through Main, Walden, and Lexington Streets, to the Square, and, after leaving the Square, up Monument Street, pass the two monuments and the bridge, and enter upon the field of Mr. George Keyes, the use of which was tendered for the occasion by the owner.

Here, on the spot where the Provincial troops made their final formation and deliberately resolved to dislodge the regulars from the bridge, a tent was to be erected for the oration and the exercises in dedication of the monument, and as near to it as the height of the river and the conformation of the ground would permit, another and larger tent for the dinner.

The success of the day depended upon the weather more than

any one was willing to acknowledge; and this fact **caused most of the difficulty** in arranging the route of the procession. **The spring was very** late, and the weather cold. Ten days before the **celebration**, **the knoll on** which the " Minute-man " stands was entirely surrounded by water, and was accessible only **by the** new bridge.

If we had been met by so unfavorable a combination of circumstances on the 19th, the procession would have been unable to pass the new monument, or, indeed, to approach it nearer than within two hundred feet; and the line of march would have been, of necessity, different in many respects.

Thus the Committee and the Chief Marshal were obliged to contemplate the possibility of material alterations in the programme, alterations which it might be necessary to make when there was no opportunity for deliberation, and when prompt action would be called for.

On the 13th, three inches of snow fell; and, as the dinner tent was to be pitched the following day, it became necessary to clear the ground. By the accommodation of the road commissioners, the men and teams employed by the town to work on the roads were set to work removing the snow from the ground that was to be occupied by the tents; and the sun came out bright and warm to assist by drying up the ground after the removal of the snow.

It was well that the spot selected for the tents was sheltered from the north winds by the hill; for, without that friendly protection, it would have been impossible for such enormous masses of canvas to withstand the blasts with which they were visited. As it was, both tents were partially lowered several times after they were first erected, in order to keep them from being blown down.

It was determined beforehand that the march around the old millpond should be omitted, if the weather or unavoidable delays should render it necessary to do so, in order to arrive at the tents at the appointed time. The actual route of the procession was thus shortened on account of unavoidable delays in formation and the embarrassment occasioned by the great crowds that blocked the streets along the line of march.

In addition to the other preparations, at the various points of historical interest, and upon the buildings now standing that were witnesses of the stirring events of the 19th of April, were placed descriptive signs. These were the work of Messrs. Edward G. Reynolds and Charles S. Richardson, acting under the direction of the

Committee on Decorations. The signs were painted on narrow strips of board in large, legible, black letters, in order that those who ran might read.

We give, for the benefit of future centennial and millennial committees, a list of the inscriptions, with a brief description of the places so designated.

HOUSE OF ADJUTANT JOS. HOSMER, 1775.

House beyond the Old South Bridge and Fitchburg Railroad crossing, now occupied by Mrs. Lydia P. Hosmer and Cyrus Hosmer.

OLD SOUTH BRIDGE.
BRITISH COMPANY STATIONED HERE 19TH OF APRIL, 1775.

Wooden bridge near Fitchburg Railroad, and house of Elijah Wood.

OLD BLOCK HOUSE, BUILT 1654.

House just west of National Bank building, occupied by Dr. H. A. Barrett.

SITE OF THE OLD JAIL.
BRITISH SOLDIERS CONFINED HERE.

This was at a point close to the north-west side of the old burying-ground on Main Street, on land of Reuben N. Rice.

SITE OF CAPT. WHEELER'S GRIST-MILL.

On the north side of the Milldam, next to the Bank, on the spot now occupied by the shop of Asa C. Collier. The old mill-stones form a substantial part of the foundation of the present building.

SITE OF CAPT. WHEELER'S STOREHOUSE.
PROVINCIAL FLOUR STORED HERE.

On the west side of Walden Street, south of the Trinitarian Church, on land of Nathan B. Stow.

MERRIAM'S CORNER.
HERE THE MINUTE MEN FROM OLD NORTH BRIDGE, WITH READING AND BILLERICA COMPANIES, ATTACKED THE BRITISH ON THEIR RETREAT.

This was about a mile and a quarter from the centre of the town, on the Boston road, at the junction of that thoroughfare with the old road to Bedford.

RESIDENCE OF DR. SAMUEL PRESCOTT,

WHO BROUGHT THE NEWS OF THE MARCH OF THE BRITISH FROM BOSTON.

House now occupied by John B. Moore on Lexington Street, in the easterly part of the town.

> "THE CONCORD ROAD TO BOSTON
> I FOR ONE
> MOST GIN'LLY OLLUS CALL IT
> JOHN BULL'S RUN."

Extract from the "Biglow Papers," posted at foot of the hill on Lexington Street, north of the house of George Heywood.

SHOP OF REUBEN BROWN,

WHERE SADDLES, CARTRIDGE-BOXES, &C., WERE MADE FOR THE PROVINCIAL ARMY.

House on Lexington Street, east side, second house north of George Heywood's, and now occupied by Mrs. Julia Clark.

OLD MEETING-HOUSE.

BUILT, 1712. ENLARGED, 1792. REMODELLED, AND TURNED HALFWAY ROUND, 1841. FIRST PROVINCIAL CONGRESS MET HERE OCT. 11, 1774. SECOND CONGRESS MET HERE MARCH 22, 1775, AND ADJOURNED FOUR DAYS BEFORE THE BATTLE AT OLD NORTH BRIDGE.

It is unnecessary to describe the location of the Church of the First Parish.

WRIGHT'S TAVERN.

PITCAIRN, STIRRING HIS BRANDY WITH BLOODY FINGER, SAID, "I HOPE TO STIR THE DAMNED YANKEE BLOOD SO BEFORE NIGHT."

House commonly known as the Jarvis House, facing the Common, a few rods north of the old meeting-house.

SITE OF OLD COURT-HOUSE, 1775.

West side of Monument Square, south of old engine-house, on land now owned by Bishop Williams.

PROVINCIAL STOREHOUSE, 1775.

House now occupied by Louis A. Surette, facing Monument Square, on the north side.

HOUSE OF ELISHA JONES, 1775.

On Monument Street, east side, now occupied by John S. Keyes. In the shed attached to the house is a bullet-hole "pierced by a British musket-ball" on the 19th of April, 1775.

An old willow tree on the same premises, planted on the 20th of April, 1775, bore the following inscription, from Holmes's "One-Horse Shay:" —

> "LITTLE OF ALL WE VALUE HERE
> WAKES ON THE MORN OF ITS HUNDREDTH YEAR
> WITHOUT BOTH FEELING AND LOOKING QUEER."

On the opposite side of the road was the following: —

OLD MANSE,
OCCUPIED BY REV. WILLIAM EMERSON, APRIL 19, 1775.

Further description is unnecessary.

HOUSE OF MAJOR JOHN BUTTRICK, 1775.

House situated on the hill west of Flint's Bridge, and lately occupied by Capt. Francis Jarvis.

HOUSE OF NATHAN BARRETT, 1775.

Situated on Punkatasset Hill, and now occupied by John B. Tileston.

HOUSE OF COL. JAMES BARRETT, 1775.

Situated about two miles from the village, in a north-westerly direction, near Angier's Mills. It is now owned by the heirs of Prescott Barrett.

In the field on the west side of the river, near the battle-ground, were posted the following memorable utterances, so closely connected with the history of the battle: —

> "FIRE, FELLOW-SOLDIERS! FOR GOD'S SAKE, FIRE!"
> MAJOR BUTTRICK.

> "I HAVEN'T A MAN THAT'S AFRAID TO GO!"
> CAPT. ISAAC DAVIS.

> "WILL YOU LET THEM BURN THE TOWN DOWN?"
> ADJUTANT HOSMER.

Just beyond the entrance to the Old Manse grounds was erected a triumphal arch with the following inscription from Lowell's "Biglow Papers:"—

"THE CONCORD BRIDGE, WHICH DAVIS, WHEN HE CAME, FOUND WAS THE BEE-LINE TRACK TO HEAVEN AND FAME."

Several other houses which were standing at the time of the fight, but, so far as is known, have no other historical connection with the day, were marked by signs bearing the date "1775."

Such were the houses of Jonathan Wheeler (the Ephraim Wheeler house), D. G. Lang (the Humphrey Barrett house), Benjamin Tolman, Walcott and Holden (the Davis house), Joel W. Walcott, (the Dr. Hunt House), Heywood and Pierce (the Yellow Block), Julia Clark (the Reuben Brown house and shop), George Heywood (the John Beaton house), and Maria K. Prescott.

At the western corner of the Hill Burying-Ground was placed a sign to indicate that "Revolutionary Heroes" were buried on the hill. So far as they could be ascertained, the graves of all the patriots who were in arms on the 19th of April, 1775, and were afterwards buried in Concord, were sought out and made conspicuous by an American flag placed over each grave.

The names of the men and their places of burial are as follows:—

OLD BURYING-GROUND.

Capt. Charles Miles.
Ensign John Barrett.
John Hosmer.
Elijah Hosmer.

HILL BURYING-GROUND.

Col. James Barrett.
Maj. John Buttrick.
Capt. Nathan Barrett.
Capt. David Brown.
Lieut. Francis Wheeler.
Rev. William Emerson.
Reuben Brown.
Stephen Barrett.
Benjamin Clark.
Ephraim Wood.
John Buttrick, Jun.
William Parkman.
Amos Melvin.
Silas Mann.

SLEEPY HOLLOW CEMETERY.

Lieut. Joseph Hosmer.
Benjamin Hosmer.
Abel Davis.

The Committee of Arrangements, at a meeting held October 17, 1874, appointed Messrs. Melvin, Shattuck, and Emerson a sub-committee to contract for and erect a liberty-pole, and raise funds for the purpose.

At the regular town meeting, November 10, the Committee was authorized to expend five hundred dollars for this purpose, that sum being in addition to the sum named in the vote under which the Committee was appointed.

The elegant flag-staff that now commands our village was built by George E. Young, of Boston, at a cost of four hundred dollars, and extends one hundred and thirty feet above the ground. Most of the remainder of the additional appropriation was expended for a flag, ball, and ropes, as will appear by the financial report of the Committee.

On the day of the celebration, the liberty-pole was beautifully dressed with flags, arranged under the immediate direction of Lieut. Commander Gorringe, and was one of the most conspicuous objects in the town. On either side, pointed up Main Street, stood the two field-pieces presented to the town by the Commonwealth, and bearing the following inscription in raised letters: —

"The Legislature of Massachusetts consecrate the names of Major John Buttrick and Capt. Isaac Davis, whose valour and example excited their fellow-citizens to a successful resistance of a superior number of British troops at Concord Bridge, the 19 of April, 1775, which was the beginning of a contest in arms that ended in American independence."

At an early day the Committee made choice of Major-General Francis C. Barlow, of New York, to act as Chief Marshal; and the following gentlemen were appointed Assistant Marshals to act as mounted aides in forming and conducting the procession: —

Col. Henry L. Higginson, Col. Charles L. Peirson, Col. Charles W. Davis, Col. Henry S. Russell, Col. William B. Storer, Col. George M. Barnard, Col. Thomas M. Wheeler, Col. Charles E. Fuller, Col. Edwin S. Barrett, Capt. William E. Wilson, Capt. Joseph Thompson, Capt. John F. Stark, Dr. Edward W. Emerson.

In addition to these assistants, a large number of gentlemen consented to act as unmounted aides, to represent the Chief Marshal in their respective towns before the day of the celebration, as well as to execute his orders respecting the movements of the procession.

While we cannot attempt, in this report, to acknowledge all the kind acts of assistance rendered us by patriotic friends all over the land, it would be a great oversight to omit all mention of the consummate ability with which the procession was planned and moved by Gen. Francis C. Barlow and his aides.

Never on the field of battle did our Chief Marshal have greater need of coolness and decision; and we venture to say that never was the exhibition of those qualities accompanied by greater success than in starting a procession such as ours within twenty minutes after the time set for it to be in motion, and conducting it safely and without delay to its destination at the opposite end of the town.

When all the events and occurrences of the 19th of April, 1875, here and elsewhere, are taken into consideration, we think that every one will feel, with the Committee, that to the promptness and efficiency of Gen. Barlow and his assistants, mounted and unmounted, is chiefly due the successful carrying out of our programme.

The following announcement was published in all the Boston daily papers during the week immediately preceding the 19th: —

CENTENNIAL CELEBRATION AT CONCORD, 19TH OF APRIL 1875.

The Committee of Arrangements of the town of Concord have made preparations for the celebration of the one hundredth anniversary of Concord Fight, 19th of April, 1775; and the citizens of all the towns locally or otherwise interested in the events of that day, and the public generally are invited to be present.

The exercises will begin with a salute of one hundred guns at sunrise.

At nine, A. M., a procession will be formed, escorted by the Fifth Regiment M V. M., and under the direction of Gen. F. C. Barlow as chief marshal. After visiting the monuments at the old North Bridge, the procession will march to a pavilion on the Provincial parade-ground, where the exercises of the dedication of the new statue will take place, consisting of an address by R. W. Emerson, and an oration upon the events of the day by George William Curtis.

At the conclusion of the oration, the company will proceed to the dinner tent on the same field. Addresses will be made at the table by many distinguished speakers.

E. R. Hoar will act as President of the Day.

The exercises will conclude with a grand ball at the Agricultural Hall in the evening.

Tickets to the dinner, $1.50; to the ball, $6; to be obtained of the Committee of Arrangements, as advertised. The number of tickets to the dinner now remaining unsold is very limited; and all persons who desire to obtain them should send their applications immediately.

Special trains will be provided on the Fitchburg and Lowell Railroads to accommodate those who desire to unite in the celebration.

By order of the Committee of Arrangements,

GEORGE KEYES, *Chairman*.

CONCORD, Mass., April 10, 1875.

SAMUEL HOAR, *Secretary*.

Following this announcement was the General Order of the Chief Marshal, which, after giving the component parts of each division of the procession, contained the following general directions : —

The different divisions will form as follows, at precisely nine o'clock, A.M., of Monday, April 19, 1875 : —

First division on Main Street, right on Thoreau Street.

Second division on Middle Street, right on Thoreau Street.

Third division on Sudbury Street, east of the railroad, right on Thoreau Street.

Fourth Division on Sudbury Street, west of railroad, right on railroad.

Fifth Division on Thoreau Street, south of Sudbury Street, right on Sudbury Street.

All persons and organizations are requested to proceed, immediately on arriving in Concord, to the points designated as above, in order that they may be placed in position by the Marshal's aides in charge of the respective divisions.

By reason of the concurrent ceremonies on the same day in the town of Lexington, it is absolutely necessary that the procession move punctually at half-past nine o'clock, and all persons and organizations not formed in their proper positions at that time will be considered as having declined the invitation to participate in the ceremonies. The available widths of the streets on which the divisions are to form are as follows : Main Street, forty feet ; Middle Street, thirty-five feet ; Sudbury Street, thirty-five feet ; Thoreau Street, thirty-five feet.

Military organizations will march in company or platoon fronts, as their commanders may designate.

All bodies of civilians marching on foot will march in ranks four abreast, with intervals of four feet between the ranks.

In order to prevent confusion in the music, the Marshal's aides (mounted) will give directions to the several bands, either directly, or through the commanders of the organizations to which the bands belong, as to the order of playing.

All ladies desiring to obtain seats at the oration will assemble at the Town Hall punctually at half-past nine o'clock, and will be conducted to the tent.

At the close of the oration and other exercises in the tent, those desiring to participate in the dinner will proceed forthwith to the tent provided for that purpose.

Col. Theodore Lyman, 191 Commonwealth Avenue, Boston, will represent the Chief Marshal in Boston until the day of the celebration, and will answer all inquiries.

All organizations or bodies proposing to join the procession, and not provided for above, are requested to communicate with Col. Lyman forthwith. It will greatly facilitate the orderly arrangement of the procession, if all persons, bodies, and organizations mentioned in the above order will communicate, as early as practicable, a statement of their numbers, and when and how they propose to reach Concord, as follows: —

Those in First Division, to Col. Henry L. Higginson, 44 State Street, Boston.

Those in Second Division, to Col. Theodore Lyman, 191 Commonwealth Avenue Boston.

Those in Third Division to Col. William B. Storer, 58 and 60 India Square, Boston.

Those in Fourth Division, to Col. Charles L. Peirson, 44 Kilby Street, Boston.

Those in Fifth Division, to Col. Charles E. Fuller, 2 State Street, Boston.

Engraved plan, showing the location of the Fitchburg Railroad station, and of the streets on which the several divisions are to form, will be sent to the assistant marshals and aides; and all persons intending to join in the procession are requested to familiarize themselves with the position of the division to which they belong, and their own place therein.

FRANCIS C. BARLOW,
Chief Marshal.

The Chief Marshal gave further directions to his assistants and to the unmounted aides in each participating town by the following printed order: —

1775.   CONCORD FIGHT.   1875.

CONCORD, MASS., April 10, 1875.

To the Unmounted Aides of the Several Towns.

Below is a sketch of the streets in the neighborhood of the railroad station, where the procession will form.

You will observe from the published order of the procession that the *official delegation* especially invited from your town (the selectmen, town officers, &c.) are in the Fourth Division, in the order indicated. This division forms on Sudbury Street, west of the railroad, right on the railroad.

Will you please see that the members of this *official* delegation clearly understand the position of their division, and their own position in it, and will you please communicate at once to Col. CHARLES L. PEIRSON (the marshal of the Fourth Division), at 44 Kilby Street, Boston, the number of such *official* delegation who will attend.

The *general* body of the citizens of your town, preceded by yourself and the town banner, and headed by such bands or organizations as you may have as escorts, will compose the Fifth Division, and will form on Thoreau Street, right on Sudbury Street.

The point where your banner will be placed will be indicated by a post on Thoreau Street, marked with the name of your town.

The delegation will form on the banner in ranks four abreast, and with intervals of four feet between the ranks.

Please communicate *at once* to Col. CHARLES E. FULLER, No. 2 State Street, the number of your *general* delegation, and whether you will have a band or any organization as an escort ; and please make your delegation as familiar as possible with these details.

Observe that the *official* delegations are in the *Fourth* Division, and the *general* delegations are in the *Fifth* Division, and communicate accordingly.

FRANCIS C. BARLOW,
Chief Marshal.

The following circular was distributed among the people of Concord by authority of the Committee of Arrangements : —

1775.   CONCORD FIGHT.   1875.

The following Order of Arrangements respecting the people of CONCORD, and their accommodation at the CENTENNIAL CELEBRATION, has been made by Major Gen. Barlow, Chief Marshal, and will be strictly adhered to.

Ladies who desire to be present at the Dedicatory Exercises and Oration are invited to assemble at the Town Hall, Monday, April 19th, at 9 o'clock, A.M., from which place they will be conducted to the Oration tent, where seats will be provided for their accommodation.[1]

The citizens of Concord, generally, and their friends who are not provided for elsewhere in the procession, are requested to assemble promptly at half-past eight o'clock, A.M., on Thoreau Street, south of Sudbury Street, where they will be formed in ranks of four, preparatory to joining in the procession.

It is hoped that the people of Concord will see the necessity of complying with the above arrangements, which have been devised for the special purpose of enabling all to be present at the Dedicatory Exercises and Oration.

No person, except ladies, will be admitted to the oration tent until after the procession has entered it.

CONCORD, April 12, 1875.

The following correspondence with Mr. George William Curtis was reported November 14, 1874, by the sub-committee on the Oration, and was accepted with unanimous approval by the general committee: —

CONCORD, MASS., Oct. 28, 1874.

GEORGE W. CURTIS, ESQ.

Dear Sir, — In behalf of the inhabitants of Concord, we cordially invite you to deliver an oration to the people of this town and their guests on the 19th of April, 1875, the centennial anniversary of Concord Fight.

In tendering you this invitation, we feel that we are giving expression to the universal desire of our people ; and we are confident, that your acceptance will give a national character to this commemoration of the deeds of our fathers.

Your obedient servants,

CHARLES H. WALCOTT,
EDWARD C. DAMON,
SAMUEL HOAR,
For the Committee of Arrangements.

---

[1] At a meeting of the General Committee, April 14, 1875, it was *voted*, "that three members of this Committee be appointed a committee to meet ladies at the Town Hall, and to conduct them to seats in the oration tent." Accordingly, such a committee was appointed, consisting of Albert F. Wood, Elijah Wood, and Marcellus Houghton, who reported at the meeting held May 8, after the celebration, that they attended to their duty, and endeavored to conduct ladies to the tent, and did conduct several ladies there ; but that others seemed unwilling to go.

WEST NEW BRIGHTON, STATEN ISLAND, N.Y.,
10 November, 1874.

GENTLEMEN, — Your invitation to deliver an oration in Concord on the centennial anniversary of Concord Fight is an honor which I cannot hesitate most gratefully and heartily, but with sincere diffidence, to accept.

With great regard, I am very respectfully yours,

GEORGE WILLIAM CURTIS.

Messrs. CHARLES H. WALCOTT,
EDWARD C. DAMON,
SAMUEL HOAR,
For the Committee.

Mr. Curtis's address forms, by his permission, a subsequent portion of this report, and speaks for itself. Words of eulogy from us to the people of Concord are unnecessary, either in praise of the orator or his work; but we think it may safely be said that, while few who heard that masterly production could fail to perceive the laborious care and reverential interest with which he had studied his subject, the earnestness, patriotism, and graceful utterance of the speaker, were felt and appreciated by all.

Mr. R. W. Emerson, having been requested to prepare an address, was appointed by the Monument Committee to speak for them at the dedication of the beautiful subject of their trust. It will be deemed no unimportant feature of our celebration that it was graced and inspired by the presence and ever youthful enthusiasm of so true a descendant of the Concord minister whose counsels and example animated his people in the opening scene of the Revolution.

Following Mr. Emerson's address, Prof. James Russell Lowell recited the noble ode which he had prepared by invitation of the Committee, a copy of which is printed hereafter in its order. It will be recognized as one of the most striking contributions to the success of the celebration, and as worthy of its distinguished author's fame. It renews the sense of obligation to him which the people of Concord have felt on other occasions.

Rev. Grindall Reynolds, the minister of the First Parish, which in 1775 was co-extensive with the town of Concord, was selected with one accord for the office of Chaplain. To him we are indebted, not only for the actual services rendered on the 19th of April, but, also, for many previous manifestations of his love for the town, and of interest in its history, which were of great assistance to the Committee in carrying out their plans. The sermon preached by Mr. Reynolds on Sunday the 18th appears, by his permission, in the subsequent pages of this report.

The Committee has attempted to show its appreciation of the services of E. R. Hoar, President of the Day, by presenting him with a letter of thanks, which was as follows: viz.,—

CONCORD, May 10, 1875.

HON. E. R HOAR.

Dear Sir,— The Committee appointed by the town to make arrangements for the celebration of the Centennial Anniversary of Concord Fight on the 19th of April, 1875, desire to express to you their sincere thanks for the able manner in which you performed the arduous duties devolving upon you as President of the Day upon that occasion.

They are aware that they are largely indebted to your untiring exertions for the success of the celebration, and feel that the town of Concord has incurred another debt of gratitude, in addition to the many it already owes you for the assistance you have so freely rendered in times past whenever it has been needed to insure the prosperity and welfare of your native town.

We are very respectfully yours, &c.,

The above letter was signed by each member of the Committee of Arrangements.

SUNDAY SERVICES.

SUNDAY SERVICES.

The scale of preparation had been such, that it was hardly possible for the assembling of guests to be confined to one day. As early, therefore, as Saturday, April 17, the Ransom Guards of St. Albans, Vermont, escorting Hon. Asahel Peck, the governor of that state, and his staff, arrived by a special train, were met at the depot by the reception committee, and marched down the main street to the hotel.[1]

On Saturday, also, in the evening, President Grant and Messrs. Fish, Belknap, Robeson, and Delano of his Cabinet, who visited New England to testify to the great national importance of the events here celebrated, came from Boston as the guests of Judge Hoar.

Friends and relatives from all parts of the country filled the houses of our towns people, and the public accommodations were stretched to their utmost.

Sunday, April 18, was a chilly, gray day. The town was quiet, considering the large numbers of visitors who filled the streets, and crowded the churches.

The Portland Mechanic Blues, escorting Hon. Nelson Dingley, jr., the governor of Maine, and his staff, arrived early in the morning; and this company, with the Ransom Guards and the Concord Artillery, attended church in the morning and afternoon.

The street decorations had been put in position. Up and down the streets, private and public buildings were festooned with flags and streamers. The two mammoth tents overlooked the town from beyond the river.

Against the vast background of the principal celebration, the modest services at the old meeting-house on Sunday attracted little public notice, yet they seem to us worthy of remembrance. The religious spirit was strong in the colonies. William Emerson, the pastor of this church, was an eye-witness of the fight at the Bridge, and by his

---

[1] This company, which made so favorable an impression during their stay in Concord, adopted the sensible course of using the special train of sleeping-cars on which they came, as a permanent camp. They thereby had ample accommodations, attended the Ball, and returned to St. Albans Tuesday morning.

example and teaching did much to strengthen the patriotism of the people of this neighborhood. In that meeting-house the first provincial congress assembled. There John Hancock was chosen to preside, and Samuel Adams was an active and influential member. From that meeting-house went forth the orders for the collection of stores and munitions of war that caused such uneasiness to the British officials; and from its pulpit, from that day to this, the lessons of patriotism, toleration, and liberty, have been inculcated by wise teachers.

It was especially fitting that there, in the presence of the chief Executive of the nation, of numerous visitors from different states, and of a large assemblage crowding the church to repletion, attention should be called with praise and prayer to the simple, the wonderful story of those men who once occupied that place, and of the birth of that nation whose freedom, and, probably, whose existence, was there made sure.

The meeting-house was handsomely decorated.

The services were the regular Sunday services of the parish,— prayer, reading of the Scriptures, singing by the whole congregation led by the Adelphi Quartette of Boston, and a discourse by Rev. Grindall Reynolds, the pastor. The singing of "America," heartily joined in by the military companies and all the congregation, was exceedingly impressive.

Mr. Reynolds's discourse was as follows: —

DISCOURSE.

BY REV. MR. REYNOLDS.

"Look upon Zion, the city of our solemnities: thine eyes shall see Jerusalem a quiet habitation. For the Lord is our judge, the Lord is our lawgiver, the Lord is our king."— ISAIAH xxxiii. 20, 22.

THE house in which we meet was first occupied for public worship in the year 1712. It was then a plain, homely building, scarcely as elegant, either in form or finish, as most of our farmers' barns. All which now adorns it — spire, porch, organ, and painted walls — are the additions of later and more luxurious times. But it was built of the great pines and oaks, which had endured the heats of a hundred summers, and breasted the storms of a hundred winters; and it was built to last. In its plainness, in its simplicity, and in its sturdiness, it was no unfit type of the strong and unpretending men who reared it, or of their sons, who, on that day, — whose morning found us colonies, whose evening left us a nation, — played their part with a rare modesty, decision, and courage. It was an old structure, therefore, when in October, 1774, it gave shelter to the First Provincial Congress of Massachusetts; weather-beaten, too, and open, no doubt, to all the breezes of heaven. For thus runs the provincial record, " In consideration of the coldness of the season, and that Congress sit in a room without fire, *Resolved*, That those members who incline thereto may sit with their hats on, while in Congress." But, plain and homely as the house was, it was the scene of most important transactions. Here, only two days after its assembling, Congress declared to Gen. Gage, in memorable phrase, that truth, which must have been new to his ears, but which is at the foundation of our national life, " that the sole end of government is the protection and security of the people. Whenever, therefore, that power, which was originally instituted to effect these important and valuable purposes, is employed to harass, distress, or enslave the people, in this case it becomes a curse." Here it was, that those military Rules and Regulations were passed, just one fortnight before the battle, which welded the scattered militia of the State into a compact army. Here, three days later, that invitation to the other New England colonies, to furnish their quota for the general defence, was voted ; and to such effect, that, almost before the retreating British troops had crossed the Charles River, companies from New Hampshire, Rhode Island, and Connecticut, were on their march to join the forces which were beleaguering Boston. And here, finally, on the 15th of April, was issued that Proclamation for a day of fasting and prayer, every one of whose sentences was an appeal to Almighty God against tyranny. This old house saw the flow and ebb of the first and the last tide of invasion which ever swept over Massachusetts soil. At seven o'clock on the 19th of April, 1775, Col. Smith halted his forces in the road and square in front of it, while, with Major Pitcairn, he climbed the steep slope of the old graveyard to take a view of the surrounding country. Four hours later, in the same road and square, that army was marching and countermarching with timid irresolution, before, at twelve o'clock, it began its well-nigh fatal retreat. Let me not forget to add, that in this old church it was, that the Rev. William Emerson, who gave up his own life to his country, from Sunday to Sunday deepened the trust, and quickened the patriotism, of the men and women of Concord by his own flaming zeal and loyalty. Could there be a better place in which to gather, that, by praise and prayer, we may fit our minds for the sacred services of remembrance and gratitude in which on the morrow we are to engage? Not within the bounds of Middlesex County is there another spot so vitally connected with the causes which preceded, and with the results which succeeded, the events of the 19th of April, 1775.

I hold that it was not of accident, that the Provincial Congress met in the meeting-houses at Concord, at Cambridge, and at Watertown. I do not believe that it was for mere convenience, that the Puritan so commonly called town-meetings, political gatherings, and all manner of public assemblies, within the walls of the houses dedicated to public worship. He did it, because he thought that they were the fit places for such things; because, to his mind and heart, all true statesmanship and all worthy government, were, equally with praise and prayer, parts of a solemn recognition and service of the sovereign God. It was not that he thought meanly of his meeting-house, but that he had grand thoughts regarding the purpose and domain of all government and law deserving the respect of a Christian man. To-morrow, eloquent lips shall portray to you the political earnestness, the sagacious statesmanship, the civic courage, and the martial valor, which conceived, which began, and which carried to a successful issue, that greatest of modern achievements, the American Revolution. Let me not trench upon that field. But the Puritan meeting-house stood, the type and symbol of other causes, which were not, perhaps, so often expressed in words, but which coursed in the very blood of the people themselves, and which gave to their words and to their deeds gravity, weight, and power. Beneath all material causes were spiritual causes, making the men of '75 what they were, and enabling them to accomplish what they did.

The colonists who came to New England did not come to advance their material interests, not to prosecute commercial enterprises, not to conquer new realms, — for none of these things, but to serve God as they felt that he ought to be served. The sovereignty of God might be to others an unmeaning phrase: to the Puritan it was a solemn reality. And he was here on these bleak shores only that he might serve God and enjoy him, now and forevermore, without let or hinderance. If any one doubts this, let him take down a volume of original Puritan letters, such as are preserved in the Prince Collection. There they are, more than two hundred years old, yellow with age, worn, and almost tattered, with much handling, — there they are; and in every one of them, in grave communication of minister to brother minister, in diplomatic note of grayheaded statesman to his peer, in letters of sober affection of husband to wife, in tender epistle of lover to his mistress, in all, and on every page of all, you will find the name of God, and the acknowledgment of his authority. That this sense of God's immediate sovereignty had lost something of its distinctness in the century and a half between Plymouth Rock and Concord Fight, one readily admits. But you read the language of him who was the brain and heart, if any one man could be, of the Revolution, and who yet was himself Puritan of Puritans, Samuel Adams, and you see that the old faith was all there in the hearts of the people, if not on their tongues. "It is the glory of the British Constitution," he says, "that it hath its foundation in the law of God." What is that but the whole doctrine of God as real sovereign, expressed in a line? The same principle is in our blood to-day. Drive a true New-England man to the wall, what is the ultimate foundation upon which he takes his stand? Not upon power, not even upon legal precedent, but upon right. And what is right, but the best we know of the will of Him who sits upon the throne of the universe, and whom we call God?

The men who marched down the hill, a hundred years ago, to the bridge, were, for the most part, sober, earnest men, — men who went to church Sundays,— men who read their Bibles and believed in them, — men who girded on their armor with the same serious and God-fearing spirit with which they went up to the house of God. What made them resolute, fearless, and, in the end, unconquerable, was that they truly thought that they were on God's side. When Major Buttrick cried out, "Fire, fellow-soldiers, for God's sake, fire!" I do not take it to have been an unmeaning phrase, or a piece of irreverence. I think that from his heart that gallant soldier believed that he stood in arms for God's sake and for the sake of the truth and the right.

It does not admit of a doubt, that this overlapping, in the Puritan mind, of true religion and true politics, shaped from the beginning the relation of the New-England colonies to royalty. The doctrine of the divine right of kings never had any great acceptance either at Plymouth, or Boston, or Salem, or Concord. A king was a servant of God; his work, the welfare of God's people. Supple courtiers might flatter a bad monarch, but not the Puritan. All the elements of resistance to oppression were in the air in 1675 just as much as in 1775: what prevented an explosion was, that as yet the colonies were too weak and insignificant to attract the attention of tyrants. The sullen opposition which was made, ten years later, to the minions of James the Second, the decision with which Nelson, Foster, and Waterhouse, the predecessors of Otis, Hancock, and Adams, arrested and sent home Sir Edmund Andros on that 19th of April, just eighty-six years before a 19th of April still more famous, prove this. Said John Higginson, plain minister of Salem, to the proud governor, "The people of New England hold their land by the grand charter of God." Not Patrick Henry, not John Adams, not any of the later patriots, ever spoke a bolder word. So when the great Boston leader said in 1771, "Kings and governors may be guilty of treason and rebellion, and they have in general, in all ages and countries, been more guilty of it than their subjects; nay, what has commonly been called rebellion in the people has often been nothing else but a manly and glorious struggle in opposition to the lawless power of rebellious kings and princes, who, being elevated above the rest of mankind, and paid by them only to be protectors, have been taught by enthusiasts to believe they were authorized by God to enslave and butcher them," he gave expression to no new thought, but only made a clear statement of an old truth, which had been embedded in the New-England consciousness from the beginning. It was John Adams, if I mistake not, who declared that the old Puritan word was, A magistrate is the servant, not of his own desires, not even of the people, but of his God.

I trace the influence of this religious interpretation of the foundation of government in that deep respect for law which grew up in the New-England mind, and which was never more characteristic of it than in the period of the Revolution. Law to it was the embodiment, in an orderly manner, of the right. Its ultimate foundation was God; its end, the welfare of the governed. Any thing which had not such a foundation and purpose was not law at all. You can in no other way than this account for the almost superstitious tenacity with which the patriotic leaders clung to the substance, and the forms, too, of legality. This tendency is evident at every step. When the Stamp-Act riot took place, by which the houses of Hutchinson and Oliver were gutted, John Adams records his painful emotions in his private diary, and Samuel Adams agreed with Mayhew, that he would rather have lost his right hand than it had happened. Not because either of them had any personal sympathy with the sufferers, but because their whole souls revolted at the idea of righting wrongs by unlawful violence. When the legislature made its final break with Gov. Gage at Salem, its last act was to declare the illegality of the proceedings of the royal officer, and the legality of its own proceedings. It was so all through. Fifty years ago, in this town, one of New England's greatest orators spoke of the events of the 19th of April as the result of an almost spontaneous rising of the people, with little or no organization or preparation behind it. I do not so read history. No doubt the spirit of the people, who were, mind, heart, soul, and conscience, on the side of what they held to be rightful authority, had much to do with the success of the struggle. But unquestionably the militia and minute-men of Concord came together that morning in obedience to a preconcerted arrangement. Unquestionably the men of Lincoln, of Acton, of Bedford, and Carlisle, and of many another town, turned their faces toward North Bridge, because such had been the previous order. It would be far nearer the truth to say, that not a minute-man was raised, not an officer chosen, not a gun forged, not a cartridge rolled, not a pound of provisions stored in a farmer's barn, except in obedience to what was held to be lawful government, resisting those who had ceased to use the sword to execute the law, and who had changed it into a deadly weapon to slay the law in the house of its friends. Law followed "the embattled farmers" as they marched down from Buttrick's Hill to the Bridge. They heard the three signal-guns fired by the enemy to summon to their aid re-enforcements. They saw the musket-balls of the British skip along the quiet surface of the river. They waited until a deadly volley had slain two of their bravest before they fired a return-shot. Why? Not because they were surprised, not because they were afraid, not, probably, because they shrank from opening a civil war, but because the law, a solemn thing then and now to a New-England man, — the law, which to them was the best expression in organized life of the divine will, commanded them not to fire until first they had been fired upon. To my mind, in all human history there is no more noble instance of the subordination of passion to duty than the silence, until the lawful order came, of those four hundred muskets at North Bridge. I cannot understand how any one can read carefully the records of the Provincial Congress of Massachusetts, and not see that the course of New England was the farthest possible remove from irregular violence and sedition; that it was the calm, orderly, resolute defence of what was solemnly believed to be alike the law of the land and the law of God against the rebellion of King George the Third and Gov. Gage, Col. Smith and Major Pitcairn, his instruments of illegality. In short, as I read history, the Revolution was that reverence of God's proper sovereignty and his righteous will, enacted into law, and brought into martial array. It was the outcome of that deep religion, which was in Puritan blood modified by the practical needs and struggles of one hundred and fifty years' life in the wilderness.

The Revolution, therefore, was no restless throwing off a yoke which galled. The fight at North Bridge was no fierce outburst of revenge. Those eight years of loss and great endurance were not given simply for selfish good of any kind: they were all parts of a steady, solemn refusal to be subject to the whims and caprices of any man, or of any body of men, be they called king or parliament, and as steady and solemn an acceptance of those charters, compacts, laws, which were the best approach which mortal wisdom had made to that absolutely wise law of God, which secures the welfare of all and each. It was this — that the Revolution was founded not on feeling, but on principle; that the forces which created it, and the forces which sustained it, were profound moral and spiritual convictions — which has made it a permanent blessing to mankind. Fifteen years later, France, in a storm of hate and defiance, rose, burst all restraints, and levelled in the dust the proudest of European monarchies. She enjoyed a long carnival of blood. Princes, nobles, spiritual peers, all who were supposed to have trampled upon the poor, and made them miserable, expiated their real or supposed crimes. But there were no principles beneath this movement; and, in ten years more, the people were back again under the power of one man. Thirty years later still, the Spanish colonies, lusting for absolute freedom, intolerant of any kind of subjection, achieved their liberty. But in their life there was no moral balance-wheel, no united, profound, grand allegiance of the whole people to any thing; and presidents, protectors, dictators, emperors, have appeared with a bewildering rapidity. But the work of the men of 1775 lasted. Says old Hooker, "That which doth assign unto each thing the kind, that which doth moderate the force and power, that which doth appoint the form and measure of working, the same we term a law." And, according to Locke, law, to be good and valid, "must be conformable to the law of nature, i.e., to the will of God." Law as good, as favorable to human welfare, as conformable to God's will, as mortals had achieved, the imperial majesty of the law — that was the principle underneath the Revolution. And to-day, in the simplest town-meeting in the smallest of New-England hamlets, you see the same principle triumphant, — the majesty of law. Without arms, without compulsion, what are legal rules in any gathering, whether of cultured or of uncultured American men. And the thought and hope of all good people is, not to subvert the law, but to perfect and purify law, and make it more and more the clear reflection of the divine will. So they who built on great principles built securely.

That other considerations, considerations of personal rights and of public and material welfare, entered, and rightly, into the conflict, no person familiar with the history of the period would for a moment deny. That meaner motives, growing out of the selfish and passionate feelings of the human heart, were mingled, as they always are mingled, with nobler motives, — that, too, is certain. But, when all proper limitations are established, it still remains true that the struggle was far more one of conscience than of interest. The deeper you search, the more thoroughly you will believe that the hopes and aims of the great men who carried the Revolution to a successful issue looked so directly to the vindication of the right, to the maintenance of the laws of nature and of God, and to the furtherance of the true welfare of God's children, that they may be properly called religious hopes and aims. And therefore it is no flight of fancy or rhetoric to say that this old meeting-house — in which our fathers transacted so much of the business of town and state, which sheltered for so many days the representatives of struggling freedom in Massachusetts, which rang with the impassioned eloquence, or was stilled by the strong logic, of some of the greatest men New England ever produced — is proper type and symbol of spiritual principles, which seemed almost to belong to Puritan blood, and which, quite as much as any material influences, created the Revolution, gave dignity to it, and made it successful.

We are on the eve of the first great centennial. To-morrow, with roar of cannon, with song of bells, with blare of martial music, with the presence of the great and honored of the land, with even files of disciplined soldiery, with long civic train, we shall seek to emphasize a great event. It is well; for no pageant can be grand enough to symbolize the blessings and greatness which have proceeded out from the brave fidelity of the humble men, who first, on the banks of yonder quiet stream, offered effectual resistance to the onset of British oppression. To-morrow, with words of splendid eulogy, with tears of sincere admiration, we shall remember those, who, in their modesty, —

> "little thought how pure a light
> With years should gather round that day;
> How love should keep their memories bright,
> How wide a realm their sons should sway."

And that is well too. For they were men whom conscience alone brought into the field, who had no ambition, except to till well the ancestral acres, to walk in peace their native plains, to rear up their children in the fear of God, and, when it was God's will, to sleep with their fathers in the old burial-place. But best of all we shall keep the day, if we remember that under the least and the greatest of the conflicts by which our nation came into existence were moral principles; that our fathers fought to achieve freedom under the law, freedom through the law, and freedom chastened and restrained by the law. We shall be children of the fathers, if we see to it that the law is to us what it was to the fathers, — the best expression of the divine will in the social state, to which man has attained. We shall be children of the fathers, if we keep human law abreast with the noblest moral and spiritual thoughts and ideas of the age, and make it the clear record of man's progress in divine wisdom, the bright transcript of God's righteous will, the steady promoter of human welfare and happiness.

At the Congregational Trinitarian Church, which is situated on a portion of the farm formerly owned and occupied by Ebenezer Hubbard, and near the place where the British soldiers broke open the storehouse of Capt. Wheeler, and destroyed the flour, appropriate services were also held.

The floral decorations were very attractive; and an American flag ornamented the pulpit. The morning services were conducted by Rev. Joseph Cook of Boston, assisted by the pastor, Rev. Henry M. Grout, who was just recovering from a protracted illness. The subject of the morning discourse was "Our Lord the World's Lord." It was listened to with great attention by a large audience.

In the afternoon, the Concord Artillery and their military guests occupied the centre of the house. Governor Peck and staff of Vermont were present; and the church was crowded. The Adelphi Quartette, and the organist who officiated at the Unitarian Church in the morning, took part in the exercises here. The musical exercises were a voluntary on the organ, anthems and hymns especially suited to the devotional character of the occasion.

The subject of the discourse, by Rev. Joseph Cook, was, "The Ultimate Results of Concord Fight." The words of the text, from Joshua ii. 1, were, "View the Land." In opening, the preacher said, "When Lafayette held in his hand the musket fired in 1775 by Col. Buttrick, at Concord Bridge, he exclaimed, 'This is the alarm gun of liberty.' The most thoughtful and patriotic poet of our own nation, however, is alarmed in 1875 as to liberty itself, and calls the United States 'the land of broken promise.' In 1813, John Adams wrote to Thomas Jefferson, ' Many hundred years must roll away before we shall be corrupted. Our pure, virtuous, public-spirited, federative republic will last forever, govern the globe, and introduce the perfection of man.' Read these great and grave words to-day to Disraeli, to Gladstone, to Carlyle, or even to John Bright, or our own congressional and municipal investigating committees, and they excite a smile. 'As to America,' said Lord Macaulay, ' I appeal to the twentieth century.' Hegel's opinion was, that, if the forests of Germany had been in existence eighty years ago, the French Revolution would not have occurred.

"It is not commonly known, even in cultivated circles, that the amount of arable soil in North and South America is greater than that in Europe, Asia, and Africa taken together. The American continent, although less than half the size of the Old World, yet contains a greater extent of productive soil. Both the promise and the perils of our future are underrated by the popular imagination." Our scandalous politics, feeble newspapers (with exceptions), and inefficient churches (with exceptions), were severely criticised. "Safe Republicanism in America must consist of four things: 1. The diffusion of liberty; 2. The diffusion of intelligence; 3. The diffusion of property; 4. The diffusion of conscientiousness. The first is the business of the government; the second, of the schools; the third, of commerce; the fourth, of the church; but the fourth is the most important of the four. Neither the education nor the conscientiousness of the masses of American citizens is commensurate with their political power. Let the family, the press, the schools join the church in the diffusion of conscientiousness; and let the ballot-box, through civil service reform, join in the same work.

"The times have not ceased to be critical. America is yet in the gristle. In America, he is not a Christian who is not a patriot, and he is not a patriot who is not a Christian."

Although on Saturday and Sunday the population of the town was more than doubled, it was interesting to notice both on those days and on the day of the celebration, as showing the depth and honesty of the spirit of patriotism that called so many together, that there was no disturbance of that public peace which is one of New England's jewels.

The streets of the village were thronged with carriages, and men and women on foot, during the whole of Sunday. The square in front of the old meeting-house was densely packed in the morning with citizens from the neighboring towns, who were unable to get inside to attend the services, and every thing betokened an event of unusual importance and interest; yet there was no noise or disorder, and the night of Sunday was as still as any night of the year.

THE CELEBRATION.

THE CELEBRATION.

THE PROCESSION.

The morning of the 19th was cold and windy, the thermometer indicating 20° Fahrenheit, much to the discomfort of the thousands, who, by a common impulse, sought by the various lines of railroad, on foot and in carriages, to reach Concord. In accordance with the established programme, a centennial salute of one hundred guns, at sunrise, from a section of Battery A, 1st Artillery, M. V. M., stationed on Nashawtuck, or Lee's Hill, opened the commemorative exercises of the day. This section of artillery was the contribution of the Commonwealth to our celebration, and, under orders from the Governor, it left Boston about eleven o'clock on the night of Sunday, and arrived in Concord before daybreak. At precisely eighteen minutes past five o'clock, the first gun was fired; and the regular succession of one hundred heavy guns called early attention to the birth of the new century of freedom.

Next in the order of the published programme was the forming of the procession. By publication in all the newspapers, by hand-bills and circulars which had been universally distributed, the Chief Marshal had endeavored to bring to the attention of every person who should come to the celebration the exact spot where each division of the procession would form, and its direction from the railroad station. Printed cards, bearing the names of the streets in full-faced type, were nailed up at every corner. Guidons, with the names of the towns thereon, were stationed where the citizens of the towns were to assemble. Every thing which ingenuity could suggest, or activity execute, had been done to further the well-nigh impossible task of marshalling an assemblage of perhaps ten thousand persons, suddenly dropped from railroad-cars and carriages, in a strange place, between the hours of eight and nine o'clock in the morning of an April day, into an orderly, systematic procession.

The large capacities of the Fitchburg and Lowell Railroads were soon tried to their utmost, and the vast numbers that came pouring into Thoreau Street showed that the estimate of an attendance of ten thousand persons was nearly six times too small. Nor was it merely curiosity, or a desire to see or form a part of a great pageant, that induced so many persons to leave their business on a day not recognized by the law as a holiday, on a day, also, that was raw and uninviting, and at personal inconvenience and exposure that in many instances were considerable, to be present in a small New England town on the anniversary of such a fight as that of April 19, 1775. But it was because patriotic memories were awakened; and the vast population that within one hundred years has sprung from those towns whose citizens were in arms on that day, the myriads of men and women of every State, from the Atlantic to the Pacific, whose ancestors are buried in the little country graveyards of eastern Massachusetts, *felt* in their veins the blood of the Revolution, and knew that the centennial celebration was a recognition by what was best in them of what was noblest in their fathers.

It was through an under-estimate, therefore, of the strength of that sentiment, that a popular attendance of only ten thousand was looked for. As it proved, the limit was the carrying capacity of the roads and railroads. And the railroads could not furnish transportation for all who desired it. From an early hour in the morning, the stations in Boston were besieged by crowds. Every ten or fifteen minutes, loaded trains were started, and at all the way-stations large numbers were gathered. The Boston and Lowell Railroad proved utterly unequal to its burden; and the resources of the Fitchburg were barely sufficient to answer the demand made on them. From eight until ten o'clock, there was hardly a moment that a train from one direction or the other was not unloading in Concord. The cars of the Framingham and Lowell Railroad were run directly to the Fitchburg station; and, in that manner, men from Lowell, from Providence, from Hartford, from Fitchburg, Worcester, and Boston, arrived simultaneously in Concord. Many, however, who had come from a distance, many who were averse to being pushed and jostled in the strife for transportation, many old men and delicate women, had to turn away from the Boston stations, and give up all hopes of participating in the celebration.

The Reception Committee had their tent pitched near the Fitchburg station in Concord, and were active in receiving distinguished guests as they arrived, and in giving directions to all who were in search of their places in the procession. A breakfast was served in Agricultural Hall, to which the veteran military organizations were conducted as they arrived.

The Governor of Massachusetts with his staff, under escort of the First Corps, of Cadets, Lieut.-Col. Edmands, reached Concord at about half-past nine, and was greeted with a salute of fifteen guns. Soon afterwards, twenty-one guns announced that the President of the United States and his Cabinet were taking their places in the line. We had hoped to march by ten o'clock, and to that end it was announced that the procession would form at nine. At half-past nine, the several divisions were nearly complete; and, to those who were punctually in their places, the slight delay in the biting wind seemed longer than it really was.

Punctually at ten o'clock the Chief Marshal gave the word, and there marched down Main Street as magnificent a pageant as was ever seen in New England. Nearly two miles in length, compact, well arranged, containing the chief national and state officers, escorted by famous military organizations, enlivened by banners and martial music, it marched through solid masses of spectators, in the following order: —

FIRST DIVISION.

Platoon of Boston Police, sixteen in number, Sergeant John H. Laskey commanding.

Medford Band, F. A. Hersey, leader, 25 pieces.

Fifth Regiment of Infantry, M. V. M. as Escort.

Colonel, Ezra J. Trull.
Lieutenant-Colonel, Charles F. King.
Major, B. Frank Stoddard.
Adjutant, Henry G. Jordan.
Quartermaster, Horace S. Perkins.
Surgeon, Edward J. Forster.
Chaplain, William T. Stowe.
Paymaster, George D. Putnam.

Company A, Boston. — Captain, John E. Phipps; First Lieutenant, John L. Curtis; Second Lieutenant, George W. Whiting. 61 men.

Company B, Somerville. — Captain, Rudolph Kramer; First Lieutenant, William S. Howe; Second Lieutenant, Charles K. Brackett. 61 men.

Company D, Boston. — Captain, Fred. B. Bogan; First Lieutenant, Michael J. Singleton. 40 men.

Company E, Medford. — Captain, Warren W. Manning; First Lieutenant, Jophamus H. Whitney; Second Lieutenant, Charles M. Green. 61 men.

Company F, Waltham. — Captain, Leonard C. Lane; First Lieutenant, Laroy Brown; Second Lieutenant, G. Frank Frost. 54 men.

Company H, Boston. — Captain, Joseph M. Foster; First Lieutenant, Frank D. Woodbury. 61 men.

Company I, Hudson. — Captain, **John F.** Dolan; First Lieutenant, Edward L. Powers; Second Lieutenant, **William** O'Donnell. 58 men.

Company K, Cambridge. — **Captain, George A.** Keeler; First Lieutenant, William L. B. Robinson; **Second Lieutenant, Henry N.** Wheeler. 61 men.

[The Fifth marched in column of sixteen platoons, Company G being absent, and Company C escorting the President in another division.]

Chief Marshal, Major-Gen. FRANCIS C. BARLOW.

Aides, Col. Henry L. Higginson, Dr. Edward W. Emerson.

George Keyes, Chairman of Committee of Arrangements; Rev. Grindall Reynolds, Chaplain of the day; Henry F. French, the father of D. C. French, the artist of the monument; and Horace Heard, the executor of Ebenezer Hubbard.

E. R. Hoar, President of the Day; George W. Curtis, Orator of the Day; James Russell Lowell, Poet of the Day; and Ralph Waldo Emerson, chosen to deliver the address of dedication.

Monument Committee and Committee of Arrangements.

Metropolitan Band; Arthur Hall, leader.

First Corps of Cadets, escorting the Governor of Massachusetts, Lieut.-Col. Thomas F. Edmands commanding.

Major, Charles P. Horton.

Captain and Paymaster, Charles E. Stevens.

Surgeon, B. Joy Jeffries.

Captain and Acting Adjutant, John D. Parker, jun.

Quartermaster, Charles C. Melcher.

Captain, William F. Lawrence.

Captain, William E. Perkins.

Captain, George R. Rogers.

First Lieutenant, Charles J. Williams.

First Lieutenant, William L. Parker.

[The Cadets numbered 110 men, and were accompanied by Cols. C. C. Holmes and John Jeffries, past commanders of the corps, and Adjutant-Gen. Cunningham.]

His Excellency, WILLIAM GASTON, Governor of Massachusetts; Col. Edward Wyman and Col. Leverett S. Tuckerman, Aides; Lieut.-Col. George H. Campbell, Military Secretary.

Judge Advocate, Gen. Patrick A. Collins; Col. A. A. Haggett and Col. Edward Gray, Governor's Aides; and Col. Charles W. Wilder, Assistant Quartermaster-General; Lieut.-Gov. Knight; Col. Whitney of the Executive Council; Col. Joshua B. Treadwell, Assistant Surgeon-General; and Col. Isaac F. Kingsbury, Assistant Adjutant-General; Col. George O. Brastow of the Executive Council; and Hon. Charles Endicott, Auditor.

Attorney-Gen. Charles R. Train, Surgeon-Gen. William J. Dale, Charles Adams, jun., Treasurer, and Oliver Warner Secretary of the Commonwealth.

Messrs. Couch, Brewster, Leland, and Turner, of the Executive Council.

Messrs. Dunn and Baker of the Executive Council, and ex-Councillors Milo Hildreth and F. H. Stickney.

Chief Justice Gray, and Associate Justices Wells and Morton, of the Supreme Judicial Court; and Charles Kimball, Sheriff of Middlesex.

Hon. Charles Devens, jun., Associate Justice of the Supreme Judicial Court of Massachusetts, and His Excellency, DANIEL L. CHAMBERLAIN, Governor of South Carolina. Judges of the Superior, Probate, and other Courts.

Col. Charles W. Davis, Aide to Chief Marshal.

American Band of Boston, Charles Thompson leader.

Newburyport Veteran Artillery Association, 100 men, in citizens' dress, with chapeau and black rosette, escorting the Legislature. — Col. Eben F. Stone, Commander; Lieuts. Warren Currier, George H. Stevens, R. M. Perley, and S. Levy; W. P. Saunders, Chief of Staff; J. P. Evans, Adjutant; George Creasy, Quartermaster's Sergeant; A. W. Thompson, Orderly Sergeant; and Joseph H. Currier and Charles Noyes, Standard-Bearers.

[Accompanying the Veterans were citizens of Newburyport, including Mayor Atkinson, Ex-Mayors Kelly, Boardman, and Graves; Mr. W. H. Huse, Collector of the Port; and other gentlemen.]

Senators Harwood and Edson, and Representatives Blunt, Tompkins, Brewer, Fitzgerald, and Burr, of the Legislative Committee of Arrangements.

Hon. George B. Loring, President of the Senate; and Hon. John E. Sanford, Speaker of the House of Representatives.

Members of the Senate and House of Representatives of Massachusetts, to the number of about 200, marching in column, four abreast.

SECOND DIVISION.

Col. Theodore Lyman, Chief of Division.

United States Marine Band of Washington, D.C., 45 men, in scarlet uniform, in charge of Lieut. Zielin of the United States Marine Corps.

Concord Artillery, Company C, Fifth Regiment, M. V. M., 60 men. Captain, George P. How; First Lieutenant, A. B. C. Dakin; Second Lieutenant, Richard F. Barrett.

[The Artillery bore the flag of the old Forty-seventh Regiment, M. V. M., in which they served during the war, and acted as special escort to the President.]

Barouche drawn by four bay horses, containing
His Excellency, ULYSSES S. GRANT,
President of the United States;
Hon. HENRY WILSON, Vice-President of the United States;
Hon. Hamilton Fish, Secretary of State; and Gen. Babcock, Military Secretary to the President.

[Flanking the barouche was a guard of twelve of the Concord Artillery.]

Hon. William W. Belknap, Secretary of War; Hon. George M. Robeson, Secretary of the Navy; Hon. Columbus Delano, Secretary of the Interior; Hon. Marshall Jewell, Postmaster-General.

Hon. James G. Blaine, Speaker of the United States House of Representatives; Hon. George S. Boutwell, United States Senator from Massachusetts; Hon. Bainbridge Wadleigh, United States Senator from New Hampshire; George W. Childs, Esq., of Philadelphia.

Hon. John H. Burleigh, Member of Congress from Maine; Hon. Charles O'Neill, Member of Congress from Pennsylvania; Hon. Stephen W. Kellogg, Member of Congress from Connecticut; Hon. M. E. Phinney of New York;

Col. Henry S. Russell, Aide to Chief Marshal.

Hon. Henry L. Dawes, United States Senator from Massachusetts; Hon. Chester W. Chapin, Hon. Rufus S. Frost, Hon. John K. Tarbox, Hon. George F. Hoar, Hon. B. W. Harris, and Hon. Charles P. Thompson, Members of Congress from Massachusetts; and W. W. Rice, Esq., of Worcester.

Hon. George F. Shepley, Judge of the Circuit Court of the United States for the First Circuit; Hon. John Lowell, Judge of the District Court of the United States for the District of Massachusetts; Hon. Daniel Clark, Judge of the District Court of the United States for the District of New Hampshire; Roland G. Usher, United States Marshal; Hon. George P. Sanger, United States Attorney; John M. Clark, Sheriff of Suffolk.

Major-Gen. Benham U. S. A.; Commodore Edward T. Nichols U. S. N.; Brevet Major-Gen. Nelson A. Miles, U. S. A.; Capt. R. W. Livermore, U. S. Engineer Corps; Commander George Brown, U. S. N.; Lieut. F. M. Wise, U. S. N., of the staff of Vice-Admiral Rowan.

THIRD DIVISION.

Col. William B. Storer, Chief of Division.

Chandler's Band of Portland, Me., 22 men.

Portland Mechanic Blues, 50 men, Capt. Charles J. Pennell, escorting His Excellency, NELSON DINGLEY, Jun., Governor of Maine, and staff.

Gen Joshua L. Chamberlin, commanding the Maine Volunteer Militia; Gen. George L. Beal, Chief of Staff; Gen. John Marshall Brown, Inspector of First Division; Gen. Joseph S. Smith; Col. A. M. Benson, Quartermaster of First Division; and Lieut.-Cols. A. W. Bradbury and George S. Follansbee, Aides-de-Camp; Roswell M. Richardson, Mayor of Portland; Hon. B. Kingsbury, jun., Ex-Mayor of Portland; Adjutant Thomas A. Roberts, formerly colonel of the Seventeenth Maine Regiment; Lieut. Henry A. Gray.

Manchester Cornet Band, 26 men.

Amoskeag Veterans of Manchester, N.H., 100 men, Major George C. Gilmore, escorting His Excellency, JAMES A. WESTON, Governor of New Hampshire, and staff.

Ex-Govs. Smyth, Stearns, and Harriman, and Hon. Person C. Cheney, of New Hampshire.

St. Albans Brigade Band, 22 men.

Ransom Guards of St. Albans, Vt., 60 men, Capt. J. W. Newton, escorting His Excellency, ASAHEL PECK, Governor of Vermont, and staff.

Judge Luke P. Poland, Ex-Member of Congress from Vermont; Hon. J. H. Page, Treasurer; Dr. George Nichols, Secretary of State; Ex-Gov. J. Gregory Smith of Vermont;

Gen. William Wells; Hon. Worthington C. Smith, Ex-Member of Congress from Vermont; Gen. John L. Barstow of Burlington; and Gen. Bigelow of St. Albans.

Capt. John F. Stark, Aide to Chief Marshal.

First Light Infantry Veteran Fife and Drum Corps, 12 men.

First Light Infantry Veteran Association of Providence, R.I., Col. W. W. Brown commanding; Major-Gen. Ambrose E. Burnside, Major; 110 men and 25 honorary members, escorting

His Honor, Lieut.-Gov. CHARLES C. VAN ZANDT, acting Governor of Rhode Island, and staff.

Fife and Drum Corps of the Putnam Phalanx.

Putnam Phalanx of Hartford, Conn., 122 men, Major Henry Kennedy, escorting His Excellency, CHARLES R. INGERSOLL, Governor of Connecticut, and staff.

FOURTH DIVISION.

Col. Charles L. Peirson, Chief of Divison.

American Brass Band, of Lowell, 22 men; Henry White, veteran drummer of Mexican War, aged seventy-three years.

Old Sixth Regiment Association, eight companies, Lieut.-Col. B. F. Watson, commanding. [The Association carried the old flags borne by the regiment in 1861, and the occasion was of double interest to it, being the fourteenth anniversary of the bloody march through Baltimore.]

Nathan Warren of Weston, a soldier of the war of 1812, and Elijah W. Stearns of Bedford. [Mr. Warren, who was eighty years old, wore his old 1812 military cap, a sort of helmet made of leather, with a high red feather plume tipped with white.]

The Massachusetts Society of the Order of the Cincinnati, 25 members, Admiral Henry Knox Thatcher, President.

The President and Fellows of Harvard University.

The Overseers of Harvard University.

The Faculty of Harvard College.

Members of the Press.

The Standing Committee of the Bunker Hill Monument Association.

The Council of the Massachusetts Historical Society.

Committee from the New England Historic-Genealogical Society.
Society of the old Guard of the war of 1812, Col. Gustavus B. Hutchinson, President;
Col. Thomas M. Wheeler and Col. George M. Barnard, jun., Aides to Chief Marshal.

Acton Brass Band, 28 pieces.

Acton Minute-Men 83 men, Capt. Aaron C. Handley [with banner bearing the inscription, "**Acton Minute-Men, April 19, 1875.**" On the reverse, "**I haven't a man that is afraid to go.**" — Capt. Davis], escorting the official delegations from the following cities and towns : —

Acton, Bedford, Billerica, Carlisle, Chelmsford, Lincoln, Littleton, Stow, Sudbury, Westford, Arlington, Belmont, Boston, Boxboro', Brookline, Burlington, Cambridge, Charlestown, Dedham, Everett, Framingham, Lowell, Lynn, Lynnfield, Maynard, Medford, Melrose, Needham, Newton, Norwood, Peabody, Pepperell, Reading, Somerville, Wakefield, Waltham, Watertown, Wayland, Weston, Winchester, Woburn.

[Accompanying the Acton delegation, in a carriage, were two of the grandchildren of Capt. Isaac Davis, — Amos W. Fitch of Cattaraugus County, New York, aged seventy-one ; and Mrs. Simon Davis of Acton, aged seventy-eight. The Wayland delegation was preceded by the Cochituate Brass Band, 24 pieces, and a company of light infantry, 80 men, Capt. D. W. Ricker.]

FIFTH DIVISION.

Col. Charles E. Fuller, Chief of Division.

Capt. James Thompson, Capt. William E. Wilson, and Capt. E. S. Barrett, Aides.

American Brass Band of Providence, R I., 28 men.

Marshal, Edward J. Bartlett.

Aides, William Wheeler, Arthur Mills, Nathan B. Smith, James L. Whitney, and William H. Brown.

Citizens of Concord, with banner of heavy white silk with inscription, "1775, Concord, 1875," and on reverse a large pine-tree.

Platoon of Salem Police.

Salem Brass Band, 21 men.

Second Corps of Cadets, 87 men, Lieut.-Col A. P. Brown commanding, escorting Hon. Henry L. Williams, Mayor, and the City Government of Salem.

Citizens of Salem.

Marshal, Capt. Cyrus Page.

Flag one hundred and thirty-eight years old, which was used in the French and Indian wars, and was carried at Concord April 19, 1775, by the Bedford Minute-Men. It has ever since been in the possession of the Page family. It bears the device of an arm with a drawn sword, and fourteen cannonballs, with the inscription "*Vincere aut morire.*" Appended to this flag was the legend, "Capt. Jonathan Wilson, killed April 19, 1775 — He died for us and Liberty."

Citizens of Bedford.

Citizens of Billerica.

Dunstable Cornet Band, mounted, 18 pieces.

Company F, Spaulding Light Cavalry, of Chelmsford, 90 men, Capt. Christopher Roby commanding, escorting

Citizens of Carlisle, under the direction of Marshal N. A. Taylor, and with a banner bearing the inscription, "Joseph Spaulding of Carlisle fired the first gun at Concord, April 19, 1775. That shot was heard round the world."

Citizens of Lincoln.

Marshal, E. B. Cobleigh.

Citizens of Boxboro', with banner, on which was inscribed, "Luther Blanchard, wounded by the first shot fired by the British."

Marshal, L. P. True.

Citizens of Everett.

Marshall, George W. Tuttle.

Citizens of Littleton with banner.

Marshal, J. P. Hildreth.

Citizens of Stow, with banner inscribed with, "The Fathers came in 1775: the Sons are here to-day, April 19, 1875."

Drum Corps.

Manchester, N.H., High School Cadets, F. H. Challis, Captain, 46 guns.

Cavalcade of citizens of Sudbury, under command of Capt. George Butterfield.

Caravan drawn by six horses, containing twenty-eight aged citizens of Sudbury.

Marshal, Luther Prescott.

Assistants, George T. Day and J. M. Chamberlain.

Citizens of Westford with banner inscribed "Lieut.-Col. Robinson, Old North Bridge, April 19, 1775. His Townsmen, April 19, 1875."

Citizens of Arlington.

Marlboro' Brass Band.

Henry Wilson Post 86, G. A. R., of Maynard; Commander, E. E. Haynes.

Citizens of Maynard.

Marshal S. A. Ranlett.

Citizens of Melrose.

Citizens of Medford.

Citizens of Brookline.

Citizens of Cambridge.

Citizens of Dedham.

Citizens of Lowell.

Citizens of Needham.

Marshal George J. Curtis.

First Regiment Band, 30 men.

Claflin Drum Corps, of Newton.

Claflin Guard, Company C, First Regiment M. V. M.; A. C. Walworth, Captain; 75 men, escorting

Mayor and City Government of Newton.

Citizens of Newton.

Reimbach's Band, 20 men.

Post 29, G. A. R. of Waltham; G. M. Hudson, Commander; 75 men, escorting Citizens of Waltham under the direction of Marshal E. Stearns.

Caravan containing ladies and gentlemen of Waltham dressed in costume of ye olden time. The caravan bore the inscription, "*Dulce et decorum est pro patria mori.*"

Citizens of Watertown.

Citizens of Norwood.

Citizens of Peabody.

Citizens of Pepperell.

Drum Corps.

Company of Continentallers from Weston, Capt. F. W. Bigelow, 50 men.

Natick Brass Band.

Citizens of Natick.

Saxonville Brass Band.

Marshal, Gen. George H. Gordon.

Post 142 G. A. R. of South Framingham, 60 men.

Citizens of Framingham, 140 men.

This division, numbering about twenty-five hundred men, closed the procession. The march was rapid on account of the cold; and it was fortunate for the spectators who covered sidewalk and roadside, and filled fences, porches, and windows, and, in some instances, were stationed even on the housetops, that the long column of six thousand or more was moved punctually and with speed. The several divisions were greeted with cheer upon cheer. The President and Cabinet, the admirable precision of the Ransom Guards, the Continental uniform of the Putnam Phalanx, the unexpected appearance of Major-Gen. Burnside marching on foot with the First Light Infantry veterans, the old Sixth veterans of the late war, the Acton Minute-Men, and several of the town delegations, gay with banners and music, were each in turn, all along the line, greeted with prolonged and renewed applause.

It had been intended to march through Walden, Heywood, and Lexington Streets, round the site of the mill-pond into which the stores and ammunition were thrown by the British, and past the old meeting-house; but in accordance with the decision, that, if necessary, the route should be shortened, that portion was omitted. This was a disappointment to some three or four thousand persons who had assembled on those streets to see the procession pass; but the change seemed unavoidable, as it was of prime necessity that the hours allotted to each of the various exercises of the day should be strictly adhered to, and only by the punctuality of starting, and the consummate skill of the Chief Marshal in conducting the procession, were we enabled to carry through the whole programme for the day without any delays.

The whole route was profusely decorated. The Committee had caused lines of flags and streamers to be thrown at frequent intervals across the streets; the houses were ornamented, according to the taste of the owners, with bunting, flags, and mottoes; and the whole appearance was that of an occasion of great triumph and rejoicing. "So gaily decked a town," said the Boston Journal of the next morning, "was never before seen in the Commonwealth." We cannot give space, however, to any minute description of the decorations on dwellings and public buildings. Suffice it to say that Main Street, Lexington Street, Walden Street, and Monument Street were fairly ablaze with festoons and color; and many houses not on the line of march were dressed in honor of the day.

As the head of the procession reached the monument grounds, the Fifth Regiment marched to the right, and, facing to the front, saluted the column as it passed through Monument Avenue, past the old monument, and the graves of the two British soldiers (over which the British ensign hung at halfmast), and across the bridge. A slight halt, and the Chairman of the Monument Committee unveiled the statue; and with as little attendant ceremony as when, one hundred years before, on that spot his prototype proclaimed himself to his countrymen and to the world, the emblematic Minute-man stood forth to command forever the admiration of men.

From the bridge to the high ground beyond is a march of only a few rods; and, at about eleven o'clock, enough of the procession had entered the tent to form, with those admitted before its arrival, an audience some four thousand in number.

The tent was capable of holding six thousand persons, and had been decorated with flags and streamers. A few seats were placed in front, near the platform, for ladies: the rest of the audience stood. The platform was raised about two feet from the ground, and was supplied with seats for two hundred persons. So many persons, other than the dignitaries for whom it was intended, crowded upon the platform as to make sitting, except for a very few, impossible.

The rear of the column had scarcely reached the square in the middle of the town, when the exercises in the tent began.

The audience was increased to the full capacity of the tent by additions from the fifth division of the procession; and multitudes who were unable to approach near enough to hear the speakers, stood in the sun, sheltered on the north by the canvas, and tried to keep themselves comfortable.

EXERCISES IN THE ORATION TEXT.

EXERCISES IN THE ORATION TENT.

Ebenezer Rockwood Hoar, the President of the Day, called the assemblage to order, and said, —

FRIENDS AND FELLOW-CITIZENS, — In this solemn hour, when the nation enters upon its second century, on the spot which was its birthplace, let us reverently ask God to be with us, as he was with our fathers.

Rev. Grindall Reynolds, the Chaplain of the Day, then offered the following

PRAYER.

Almighty God, Giver of every good, from whose kind providence every blessing and joy, all honor, all greatness, and all success, do proceed, we praise and magnify thy holy name. We rejoice in this bright, beautiful morning, which smiles upon us, as we meet to remember the great, pure, and honorable deeds which have made this spot sacred.

We rejoice, in this great presence, that the sons and daughters of this town, from the east and from the west, have gathered together to refresh heart and soul by tearful remembrance and by glad thanksgiving. We rejoice in the presence of this great multitude, who have come up hither from all the towns and states of a great and free country, which has grown up since the day we commemorate. We rejoice in the presence of these citizen soldiers, representatives of the men who came forth from farm-houses, from counting-rooms, from all the places of human duty and labor, to offer up their lives a sacrifice to liberty.

We rejoice in the presence of those who have been called to rule over this country, in the presence of him who is the chief magistrate of this great nation, and of all who, in their various places, seek to do their part in executing the laws, in promoting the welfare of the people, and in building this nation up to a greater glory and to a purer righteousness. We thank thee for the memories which we cherish of the plain, simple men, who, not for any worldly honors, but for conscience' sake, and God's sake, confronted the enemy in that hour of fiery trial.

And, as we gather to deepen and make sacred these recollections of their courage and sacrifice, we rejoice that thy goodness has blessed their toils, and from a little people built us up to be a great nation. With hearts full of gratitude, we bow, and say, " Not unto us the glory, but unto thy great name, O Lord of Hosts." Prepare our hearts for the words which shall be spoken to-day, for the eloquent utterances which the memories and the hopes of the hour shall call forth. Prepare us for the sacred influences which shall steal into our hearts, that, when this day is over, we may return to our homes, here or in distant places, to do our duty, to be good citizens, honestly and nobly to fill our places in the world. And as thy blessing comes to us in the beauty of this morning, may it be with us throughout the day, and may it go with us to our homes. We ask and offer all in the name of Jesus Christ, our Lord. Amen.

The President of the Day then said,—

In the presence of the President and Vice-President of the United States, attended by the Cabinet, in the presence of the Governor, the Executive Council, and the Legislature of Massachusetts, in the presence of the Governor of each of the New England states, we have to-day dedicated a statue to the memory of the first soldiers of the Revolution upon the spot where the first order was given to the soldiers of the people to fire upon the soldiers of the king. In appropriate notice of that act, you will be addressed for a few moments by Mr. Emerson.

Mr. Emerson was received with great applause, after which he delivered the following : —

ADDRESS.

FELLOW-CITIZENS, — Ebenezer Hubbard, a farmer who inherited land in this village on which the British troops committed depredation, and who had a deep interest in the history of the raid, erected, many years ago, a flagstaff on his ground, and never neglected to hoist the stars and stripes on the Nineteenth of April, and the Fourth of July. It grieved him deeply that yonder monument, erected by the town in 1836, should have been built on the ground on which the enemy stood in the Concord Fight, instead of on that which the Americans occupied; and he bequeathed in his will one thousand dollars to the town of Concord, on condition that a monument should be erected on the identical ground occupied by our minute-men and militia on that day; and an additional sum of six hundred dollars, on the condition that the town should build a foot-bridge across the river, on the site where the old bridge stood in 1775. The late Mr. Stedman Buttrick having given the necessary piece of land on the other side of the river, the town accepted the legacy of Mr. Hubbard, built the bridge, and employed Daniel C. French to prepare a statue to be erected on the specified spot. Meanwhile the United States Congress gave to this town ten bronze cannon to furnish the artist with fit material to complete his work. The finished statue is before you: it was approved by the town, and to-day it speaks for itself. The sculptor has rightly conceived the proper emblems of the patriot farmer, who, at the morning alarm, left his plough to grasp his gun. He has built no dome over his work, believing that blue sky makes the best canopy. The statue is the first serious work of our young townsman, who is now in Italy to pursue his profession.

In the year 1775, we had many enemies and many friends in England; but our one benefactor was King George the Third. The time had arrived for the political severance of America, that it might play its part in the history of this globe; and the inscrutable Divine Providence gave an insane king to England. In the resistance of the colonies, he alone was immovable on the question of force. England was so dear to us, that the colonies could only be absolutely united by violence from England; and only one man could compel the resort to violence. So the king became insane. Parliament wavered; Lord North wavered; all the ministers wavered; but the king had the insanity of one idea. He was immovable, he insisted on the impossible: so the army was sent, America was instantly united, and the nation born. On the 19th of April, eight hundred soldiers with hostile purpose were sent hither from Boston: on their way, they made the previous attack on Lexington, then continued their march hither to search for and capture military stores. Three companies were left at this bridge, two of which were drawn back towards the hill close behind us. The number of our own militia companies is believed to have been from two hundred and fifty to three hundred men.

In some memorable events in history, Nature has seemed to sympathize with Man. We mark in the rude air and the still brown fields of this morning the slow departure of winter; but on the same day of the year 1775, a rare forwardness of the spring is recorded, marked by the fact that "the rye waved on the 19th of April." Shall we believe that the patriotism of the people was so hot, that it melted the snow?

We gladly see among us this morning the representatives of Acton, Bedford, Lincoln, and Carlisle, four towns once included in our town limits, whose citizens were mindful of their mother-town, and risked their lives for her on the memorable day we celebrate. Isaac Davis of Acton was the first martyr; Abner Hosmer of Acton, the next. In all noble action, we say 'tis only the first step that costs.

Who will carry out the rule of right must take his life in his hand.

We have no need to magnify the facts. Only two of our men were killed at the bridge, and four others wounded. But here the British army was first fronted, and driven back; and if only two men, or only one man, had been slain, it was the first victory. The thunderbolt falls on an inch of ground; but the light of it fills the horizon. The British instantly retreated. We had no electric telegraph; but the news of this triumph of the farmers over the King's troops flew through the country, to New York, to Philadelphia, to Kentucky, to the Carolinas, with speed unknown before, and ripened the colonies to inevitable decision.

This sharp beginning of real war was followed, sixty days later, by the battle of Bunker Hill; then by General Washington's arrival in Cambridge, and the raising of his redoubts on Dorchester Heights. In ten months and twenty-five days from the death of Isaac Davis and Abner Hosmer, one hundred and twenty vessels loaded with General Howe and his army (eight thousand men), with all their effects, sailed out of Boston Harbor never to return. It is a proud and tender story. I challenge any lover of Massachusetts to read the fifty-ninth chapter of Bancroft's History* without tears of joy.

At the conclusion of Mr. Emerson's address, the President of the Day said, —

"FELLOW-CITIZENS, — We have the pleasure to-day, not announced beforehand, of the presence of this our Middlesex County poet, the poet of Cambridge and Concord; and I introduce to you, with great delight, James Russell Lowell."

---

* History of the United States, vol. viii. chap. liv.

Mr. Lowell then read the following: —

ODE.

I.

Who cometh over the hills,
Her garments with morning sweet,
The dance of a thousand rills
Making music before her feet?
Her presence freshens the air;
Sunshine steals light from her face;
The leaden footstep of Care
Leaps to the tune of her pace,
Fairness of all that is fair,
Grace at the heart of all grace,
Sweetener of hut and of hall,
Bringer of life out of nought,
Freedom, oh, fairest of all
The daughters of Time and Thought!

II.

She cometh, cometh to day:
Hark! hear ye not her tread,
Sending a thrill through your clay,
Under the sod there, ye dead,
Her nurselings and champions?
Do ye not hear, as she comes,
The bay of the deep-mouthed guns,
The gathering buzz of the drums?
The bells that called ye to prayer,
How wildly they clamor on her,
Crying, "She cometh! prepare
Her to praise and her to honor,
That a hundred years ago
Scattered here in blood and tears
Potent seeds wherefrom should grow
Gladness for a hundred years?"

III.

Tell me, young men, have ye seen
Creature of diviner mien
For true hearts to long and cry for,
Manly hearts to live and die for?
What hath she that others want?
Brows that all endearments haunt,
Eyes that make it sweet to dare,
Smiles that glad untimely death,
Looks that fortify despair,
Tones more brave than trumpet's breath;
Tell me, maidens, have ye known
Household charm more sweetly rare,
Grace of woman ampler blown,
Modesty more debonair,
Younger heart with wit full grown?
Oh for an hour of my prime,
The pulse of my hotter years,
That I might praise her in rhyme
Would tingle your eyelids to tears,
Our sweetness, our strength, and our star,
Our hope, our joy, and our trust,
Who lifted us out of the dust,
And made us whatever we are!

IV.

Whiter than moonshine upon snow
Her raiment is, but round the hem
Crimson stained; and, as to and fro
Her sandals flash, we see on them,
And on her instep veined with blue,
Flecks of crimson, on those fair feet,
High-arched, Diana-like, and fleet,
Fit for no grosser stain than dew:
Oh, call them rather chrisms than stains,
Sacred and from heroic veins!
For, in the glory-guarded pass,
Her haughty and far-shining head
She bowed to shrive Leonidas
With his imperishable dead;
Her, too, Morgarten saw,
Where the Swiss lion fleshed his icy paw;

She followed Cromwell's quenchless star
Where the grim Puritan tread
Shook Marston, Nasby, and Dunbar :
Yea, on her feet are dearer dyes
Yet fresh, nor looked on with untearful eyes.

v.

Our fathers found her in the woods
Where Nature meditates, and broods
The seeds of unexampled things
Which Time to consummation brings
Through life and death and man's unstable moods.
They met her here, not recognized,
A sylvan huntress clothed in furs,
To whose chaste wants her bow sufficed,
Nor dreamed what destinies were hers.
She taught them bee-like to create
Their simpler forms of Church and State ;
She taught them to endue
The past with other functions than it knew,
And turn in channels strange the uncertain stream of Fate ;
Better than all, she fenced them in their need
With iron-handed Duty's sternest creed,
'Gainst Self's lean wolf that ravens word and deed.

vi.

Why cometh she hither to-day
To this low village of the plain
Far from the Present's loud highway,
From Trade's cool heart and seething brain ?
Why cometh she ? She was not far away.
Since the soul touched it, not in vain,
With pathos of immortal gain,
'Tis here her fondest memories stay.
She loves yon pine-bemurmured ridge
Where now our broad-browed poet sleeps,
Dear to both Englands ; near him he
Who wore the ring of Canace ;
But most her heart to rapture leaps
Where stood that era-parting bridge,
O'er which, with footfall still as dew,
The Old Time passed into the New ;
Where, as your stealthy river creeps,

He whispers to his listening weeds
Tales of sublimest homespun deeds.
Here English law and English thought
'Gainst the selfwill of England fought;
And here were men (co-equal with their fate),
Who did great things, unconscious they were great.
They dreamed not what a die was cast
With that first answering shot; what then?
There was their duty; they were men
Schooled the soul's inward gospel to obey,
Though leading to the lion's den.
They felt the habit-hallowed world give way
Beneath their lives, and on went they,
Unhappy who was last.
When Buttrick gave the word,
That awful idol of the unchallenged Past,
Strong in their love, and in their lineage strong,
Fell crashing: if they heard it not,
Yet the earth heard,
Nor ever hath forgot,
As on from startled throne to throne,
Where Superstition sate on conscious Wrong,
A shudder ran of some dread birth unknown.
Thrice venerable spot!
River more fateful than the Rubicon!
O'er those red planks, to snatch her diadem,
Man's Hope, star-girdled, sprang with them,
And over ways untried the feet of Doom strode on.

VII.

Think you these felt no charms
In their gray homesteads and embowered farms?
In household faces waiting at the door
Their evening step should lighten up no more?
In fields their boyish steps had known?
In trees their fathers' hands had set,
And which with them had grown,
Widening each year their leafy coronet?
Felt they no pang of passionate regret
For those unsolid goods that seem so much our own?
These things are dear to every man that lives,
And life prized more for what it lends than gives.
Yea, many a tie, by iteration sweet,
Strove to detain their fatal feet;

And yet the enduring half they chose,
Whose choice decides a man life's slave or king,
The invisible things of God before the seen and known
Therefore their memory inspiration blows
With echoes gathering on from zone to zone ;
For manhood is the one immortal thing
Beneath Time's changeful sky,
And, where it lightened once, from age to age,
Men come to learn, in grateful pilgrimage,
That length of days is knowing when to die.

VIII.

What marvellous change of things and men !
She, a world-wandering orphan then,
So mighty now !   Those are her streams
That whirl the myriad, myriad wheels
Of all that does, and all that dreams,
Of all that thinks, and all that feels,
Through spaces stretched from sea to sea ;
By idle tongues and busy brains,
By who doth right, and who refrains,
Hers are our losses and our gains ;
Our maker and our victim she.

IX.

Maiden half mortal, half divine,
We triumphed in thy coming ; to the brinks
Our hearts were filled with pride's tumultuous wine ;
Better to-day who rather feels than thinks.
Yet will some graver thoughts intrude,
And cares of sterner mood ;
They won thee : who shall keep thee ?   From the deeps
Where discrowned empires o'er their ruins brood,
And many a thwarted hope wrings its weak hands and weeps,
I hear the voice as of a mighty wind
From all heaven's caverns rushing unconfined,
" I, Freedom, dwell with Knowledge : I abide
With men whom dust of faction cannot blind
To the slow tracings of the Eternal Mind,
With men by culture trained and fortified,
Who bitter duty to sweet lusts prefer,
Fearless to counsel and obey.

Conscience my sceptre is, and law my sword,
Not to be drawn in passion or in play,
But terrible to punish and deter;
Implacable as God's word,
Like it, a shepherd's crook to them that blindly err.
Your firm-pulsed sires, my martyrs and my saints,
Shoots of that only race whose patient sense
Hath known to mingle flux with permanence,
Rated my chaste denials and restraints
Above the moment's dear-paid paradise:
Beware lest, shifting with Time's gradual creep,
The light that guided shine into your eyes.
The envious Powers of ill nor wink nor sleep.
Be therefore timely wise,
Nor laugh when this one steals, and that one lies,
As if your luck could cheat those sleepless spies,
Till the deaf Fury comes your house to sweep!"
I hear the voice, and unaffrighted bow;
Ye shall not be prophetic now,
Heralds of ill, that darkening fly
Between my vision and the rainbowed sky,
Or on the left your hoarse forebodings croak
From many a blasted bough
On Yggdrasil's storm-sinewed oak,
That once was green, Hope of the West, as thou:
Yet pardon if I tremble while I boast;
For thee I love as those who pardon most.

X.

Away, ungrateful doubt, away!
At least she is our own to-day.
Break into rapture, my song,
Verses, leap forth in the sun,
Bearing the joyance along
Like a train of fire as ye run!
Pause not for choosing of words,
Let them but blossom and sing
Blithe as the orchards and birds
With the new coming of spring!
Dance in your jollity, bells;
Shout, cannon; cease not, ye drums;
Answer, ye hillside and dells;
Bow, all ye people! She comes,

Radiant, calm-fronted, as when
She hallowed that April day.
Stay with us! Yes, thou shalt stay,
Softener and strengthener of men,
Freedom, not won by the vain,
Not to be courted in play,
Not to be kept without pain.
Stay with us! Yes, thou wilt stay,
Handmaid and mistress of all,
Kindler of deed and of thought,
Thou that to hut and to hall
Equal deliverance brought!
Souls of her martyrs, draw near,
Touch our dull lips with your fire,
That we may praise without fear
Her our delight, our desire,
Our faith's inextinguishable star,
Our hope, our remembrance, our trust,
Our present, our past, our to be,
Who will mingle her life with our dust,
And makes us deserve to be free!

The President of the Day then said, —

A man whose studious youth was passed near the Old North Bridge in Concord, and whose eloquent words have since been known throughout the nation, will address you as the orator of the day, — George William Curtis, once of Concord, now of New York. Before he begins, as you may not all be in the tent at the dinner, I will hold up for this audience to see, all that is left of the sword that Isaac Davis carried at Concord North Bridge. There is about a foot gone; but it would only require him to have taken one step farther forward, which he would willingly have done.

Loud applause followed these remarks; and Mr. Curtis was also warmly applauded as he rose. After acknowledging the greeting of the audience, he delivered the following:

ORATION.

We are fortunate that we behold this day. The heavens bend benignly over; the earth blossoms with renewed life; and our hearts beat joyfully together with one emotion of filial gratitude and patriotic exultation. Citizens of a great, free, and prosperous country, we come hither to honor the men, our fathers, who, on this spot and upon this day, a hundred years ago, struck the first blow in the contest which made that country independent. Here beneath the hills they trod, by the peaceful river on whose shores they dwelt, amidst the fields that they sowed and reaped, proudly recalling their virtue and their valor, we come to tell their story, to try ourselves by their lofty standard to know if we are their worthy children, and, standing reverently where they stood and fought and died, to swear before God and each other, in the words of him upon whom in our day the spirit of the Revolutionary fathers visibly descended, that government of the People, by the People, for the People, shall not perish from the earth.

This ancient town, with its neighbors who share its glory, has never failed fitly to commemorate this great day of its history. Fifty years ago, while some soldiers of the Concord fight were yet living,— twenty-five years ago, while still a few venerable survivors lingered,— with prayer and eloquence and song you renewed the pious vow. But the last living link with the Revolution has long been broken. Great events and a mightier struggle have absorbed our own generation. Yet we who stand here to-day have a sympathy with the men at the old North Bridge, which those who preceded us here at earlier celebrations could not know. With them, war was a name and a tradition. So swift and vast had been the change and the development of the country, that the Revolutionary clash of arms was already vague and unreal, and Concord and Lexington seemed to them almost as remote and historic as Arbela and Sempach. When they assembled to celebrate this day, they saw a little group of tottering forms, eyes from which the light was fading, arms nerveless and withered, thin white hairs that fluttered in the wind; they saw a few venerable relics of a vanished age, whose pride was, that, before living memory, they had been minute-men of American Independence. But with us how changed! War is no longer a tradition half romantic and obscure. It has ravaged how many of our homes! it has wrung how many of the hearts before me! North and South we know the pang. Our common liberty is consecrated by a common sorrow. We do not count around us a few feeble veterans of the contest; but we are girt with "a cloud of witnesses." We are surrounded everywhere by multitudes in the vigor of their prime. Behold them here to-day sharing in these pious and peaceful rites, — the honored citizens, legislators, magistrates, yes, the Chief Magistrate of the republic, — whose glory it is that they were minute-men of American liberty and union. These men of to-day interpret to us with resistless eloquence the men and the times we commemorate. Now, if never before, we understand the Revolution. Now we know the secret of those old hearts and homes. We can measure the sacrifice, the courage, the devotion; for we have seen them all. Green hills of Concord, broad fields of Middlesex, that heard the voice of Hancock and of Adams, you heard, also, the call of Lincoln and of Andrew; and your Ladd and Whitney, your Prescott and Ripley and Melvin, have revealed to us more truly the Davis and the Buttrick, the Hosmer and the Parker, of a hundred years ago.

The story of this old town is the history of New England. It shows us the people and the institutions that have made the American republic. Concord was the first settlement in New England above tide-water. It was planted directly from the mother-country, and was what was called a mother-town, the parent of other settlements throughout the wilderness. It was a military post in King Philip's war; and two hundred years ago — just a century before the minute-men whom we commemorate — the militia of Middlesex were organized as minute-men against the Indians. It is a Concord tradition, that in those stern days, when the farmer tilled these fields at the risk of his life, Mary Shepard, a girl of fifteen, was watching on one of the hills for the savages, while her brothers threshed in the barn. Suddenly the Indians appeared, slew the brothers, and carried her away. In the night, while the savages slept, she untied a horse which they had stolen, slipped a saddle from under the head of one of her captors, mounted, fled, swam the Nashua River, and rode through the forest home. Mary Shepard was the true ancestor of the Concord matrons who share the fame of this day, — of Mrs. James Barrett, of the Widow Brown, of Mrs. Amos Wood, and Hannah Burns, with the other faithful women whose self-command, and ready wit and energy, on this great morning, show that the mothers of New England were like the fathers, and that equally in both their children may reverence their own best virtues.

A little later than Philip's war, one hundred and eighty-six years ago last night, while some of the first settlers of Massachusetts Bay still lingered, when the news came that King

James the Second had been dethroned, a company marched from this town, and joined that general uprising of the colony which the next day, this very day, with old Simon Bradstreet at its head, deposed Sir Edmund Andros, the king's governor, and restored the ancient charter of the colony. "We demand only the traditional rights of Englishmen," said the English nobles, as they seated William and Mary upon the throne. "We ask nothing more," said the freemen of Concord, as they helped to dissolve royal government in America, and returned to their homes. Eighty-five years later, the first Provincial Congress, which had been called to meet at Concord, if, for any reason, the General Court at Salem were obstructed, assembled in the old meeting-house on the 11th of October, 1774, the first independent legislature in Massachusetts, in America; and from that hour to this the old mother-town has never forgotten the words, nor forsworn the faith, of the Revolution, which had been proclaimed here six weeks before: "No danger shall affright, no difficulties intimidate us; and if, in support of our rights, we are called to encounter even death, we are yet undaunted, sensible that he can never die too soon who lays down his life in support of the laws and liberties of his country."

But the true glory of Concord, as of all New England, was the town meeting, the nursery of American Independence. When the Revolution began, of the eight millions of people then living in Old England, only one hundred and sixty thousand were voters; while in New England the great mass of free male adults were electors. And they had been so from the landing at Plymouth. Here in the wilderness the settlers were forced to govern themselves. They could not constantly refer and appeal to another authority twenty miles away through the woods. Every day brought its duty, that must be done before sunset. Roads must be made, schools built, young men trained to arms against the savage and the wild-cat, taxes must be laid and collected for all common purposes, preaching must be maintained; and who could know the time, the means, and the necessity, so well as the community itself? Thus each town was a small but perfect republic, as solitary and secluded in the New England wilderness as the Swiss cantons among the Alps. No other practicable human institution has been devised or conceived to secure the just ends of local government so felicitous as the town meeting. It brought together the rich and the poor, the good and the bad, and gave character, eloquence, and natural leadership full and free play. It enabled superior experience and sagacity to govern; and virtue and intelligence alone are rulers by divine right. The Tories called the resolution for committees of correspondence the source of the rebellion; but it was only a correspondence of town meetings. From that correspondence came the confederation of the colonies. Out of that arose the closer, majestic union of the Constitution, the greater phœnix born from the ashes of the lesser; and the national power and prosperity to-day rest securely only upon the foundation of the primary meeting. That is where the duty of the citizen begins. Neglect of that is disloyalty to liberty. No contrivance will supply its place, no excuse absolve the neglect; and the American who is guilty of that neglect is as deadly an enemy of his country as the British soldier a century ago.

But here and now I cannot speak of the New England town meeting without recalling its great genius, the New-Englander in whom the Revolution seemed to be most fully embodied, and the lofty prayer of whose life was answered upon this spot and on this day. He was not eloquent like

Otis, nor scholarly like Quincy, nor all-fascinating like Warren, yet bound heart to heart with these great men, his friends, the plainest, simplest, austerest, among them, he gathered all their separate gifts, and, adding to them his own, fused the whole in the glow of that untiring energy, that unerring perception, that sublime will, which moved before the chosen people of the colonies a pillar of cloud by day, of fire by night. People of Massachusetts, your proud and grateful hearts outstrip my lips in pronouncing the name of Samuel Adams. Elsewhere to-day, nearer the spot where he stood with his immortal friend Hancock a hundred years ago this morning, a son of Massachusetts, who bears the name of a friend of Samuel Adams, and whose own career has honorably illustrated the fidelity of your State to human liberty, will pay a fitting tribute to the true American tribune of the people, — the father of the Revolution, as he was fondly called. But we also are his children, and must not omit our duty.

Until 1768, Samuel Adams did not despair of a peaceful issue of the quarrel with Great Britain. But when, in May of that year, the British frigate "Romney" sailed into Boston harbor, and her shotted guns were trained upon the town, he saw that the question was changed. From that moment, he knew that America must be free, or slave; and the unceasing effort of his life by day and night, with tongue and pen, was to nerve his fellow-colonists to strike when the hour should come. On that gray December evening, two years later, when he rose in the Old South, and in a clear, calm voice said, "This meeting can do nothing more to save the country," and so gave the word for the march to the tea-ships, he comprehended more clearly, perhaps, than any man in the colonies, the immense and far-reaching consequences of his words. He was ready to throw the tea overboard, because he was ready to throw overboard the King and Parliament of England.

During the ten years from the passage of the Stamp Act to the day of Lexington and Concord, this poor man, in an obscure provincial town beyond the sea, was engaged with the British ministry in one of the mightiest contests that history records. Not a word in parliament that he did not hear, not an act in the cabinet that he 'did not see. With brain and heart and conscience all alive, he opposed every hostile order in council with a British precedent, and arrayed against the Government of Great Britain the battery of principles impregnable with the accumulated strength of centuries of British conviction. The cold Grenville, the brilliant Townsend, the obsequious North, the reckless Hillsborough, the crafty Dartmouth, all the ermined and coroneted chiefs of the proudest aristocracy in the world, derided, declaimed, denounced, laid unjust taxes, and sent troops to collect them, cheered loudly by a servile parliament, the parasite of a headstrong king; and the plain Boston Puritan laid his finger on the vital point of the tremendous controversy, and held to it inexorably king, lords, commons, the people of England, and the people of America. Entrenched in his own honesty, the king's gold could not buy him; enshrined in the love of his fellow-citizens, the king's writ could not take him: and when, on this morning, the king's troops marched to seize him, his sublime faith saw beyond the clouds of the moment the rising sun of the America that we behold; and careless of himself, mindful only of his country, he exultingly exclaimed, " Oh, what a glorious morning! "

Yet this man held no office but that of clerk of the assembly, to which he was yearly elected, and that of constant moderator of the town meeting. That was his mighty weapon. The town meeting was the alarm-bell with which he aroused the continent: it was the rapier with which he fenced with the ministry: it was the claymore with which he smote their counsels: it was the harp of a thousand strings that he swept into a burst of passionate defiance, or an electric call to arms, or a proud pæan of exulting triumph, defiance, challenge, and exultation — all lifting the continent to independence. His indomitable will, and command of the popular confidence, played Boston against London, the provincial town meeting against the royal parliament, Faneuil Hall against St. Stephen's. And as long as the American town meeting is known, its great genius will be revered, who with the town meeting overthrew an empire. So long as Faneuil Hall stands, Samuel Adams will not want his most fitting monument; and, when Faneuil Hall falls, its name with his will be found written as with a sunbeam upon every faithful American heart.

The first imposing armed movement against the colonies, on the 19th of April, 1775, did not, of course, take by surprise a people so prepared. For ten years they had seen the possibility, for five years the probability, and for at least a year, the certainty, of the contest. They quietly organized, watched, and waited. The royal governor, Gage, was a soldier; and he had read the signs of the times. He had fought with provincial troops at the bloody ambuscade of Braddock; and he felt the full force of the mighty determination that exalted New England. He had about four thousand effective troops, trained veterans, with brilliant officers, who despised and ridiculed the Yankee militia. Massachusetts had provided for a constitutional army of fifteen thousand men. Minute companies were everywhere organized, and military supplies were deposited at convenient towns. Everybody was on the alert. Couriers were held ready to alarm the country, should the British march, and wagons to remove the stores. In the early spring, Gage sent out some of his officers as spies; and two of them came in disguise as far as Concord. On the 22d of March, the Provincial Congress met in this town, and made the last arrangements for a possible battle, begging the militia and minute-men to be ready, but to act only on the defensive.

As the spring advanced, it was plain that some movement would be made; and on Monday, the 17th of April, the Committee of Safety ordered part of the stores deposited here to be removed to Sudbury and Groton, and the cannon to be secreted. On Tuesday, the 18th, Gage, who had decided to send a force to Concord to destroy the stores, picketed the roads from Boston into Middlesex to prevent any report of the intended march from spreading into the country. But the very air was electric. In the tension of the popular mind, every sound and sight was significant. It was part of Gage's plan to seize Hancock and Adams, who were at Lexington; and, on the evening of the 18th, the Committee of Safety, at Cambridge, sent them word to beware, for suspicious officers were abroad. A British grenadier, in full uniform, went into a shop in Boston. He might as well have proclaimed that an expedition was on foot. In the afternoon, one of the governor's grooms strolled into a stable where John Ballard was cleaning a horse. John Ballard was a son of liberty; and when the groom idly remarked, in nervous English, that "there would be hell to pay to-morrow," John's heart leaped, and his hand shook; and, asking the groom to finish cleaning the horse, he ran to a friend, who carried the news straight to Paul Revere, who told him he had already heard it from two other persons.

That evening, at ten o'clock, eight hundred British troops,

under Lieut.-Col. Smith, took boat at the foot of the Common, and crossed to the Cambridge shore. Gage thought that his secret had been kept; but Lord Percy, who had heard the people say on the Common that the troops would miss their aim, undeceived him. Gage instantly ordered that no one should leave the town. But Dr. Warren was before him; and, as the troops crossed the river, William Dawes, with a message from Warren to Hancock and Adams, was riding over the Neck to Roxbury, and Paul Revere was rowing over the river farther down to Charlestown, having agreed with his friend Robert Newman to show lanterns from the belfry of the Old North Church —

"One, if by land, and two, if by sea" —

as a signal of the march of the British. Already the moon was rising; and, while the troops were stealthily landing at Lechmere Point, their secret was flashed out into the April night; and Paul Revere, springing into the saddle upon the Charlestown shore, spurred away into Middlesex.

"How far that little candle throws his beams!"

The modest spire yet stands, reverend relic of the old town of Boston, — of those brave men and of their deeds. Startling the land that night with the warning of danger, let it remind the land forever of the patriotism with which that danger was averted, and for our children, as for our fathers, still stand secure, the Pharos of American liberty.

It was a brilliant April night. The winter had been unusually mild, and the spring very forward. The hills were already green; the early grain waved in the fields; and the air was sweet with blossoming orchards. Already the robins whistled, the bluebird sang, and the benediction of peace rested upon the landscape. Under the cloudless moon the soldiers silently marched, and Paul Revere swiftly rode, galloping through Medford and West Cambridge, rousing every house as he went, spurring for Lexington, and Hancock and Adams, and evading the British patrols who had been sent out to stop the news. Stop the news! Already the village church bells were beginning to ring the alarm, as the pulpits beneath them had been ringing for many a year. In the awakening houses, lights flashed from window to window. Drums beat faintly far away and on every side. Signal-guns flashed and echoed. The watch-dogs barked, the cocks crew. Stop the news! Stop the sunrise! The murmuring night trembled with the summons so earnestly expected, so dreaded, so desired. And as, long ago, the voice rang out at midnight along the Syrian shore, wailing that great Pan was dead, but in the same moment the choiring angels whispered, "Glory to God in the highest, for Christ is born," so, if the stern alarm of that April night seemed to many a wistful and loyal heart to portend the passing glory of British dominion, and the tragical chance of war, it whispered to them with prophetic inspiration, "Good-will to men: America is born!"

There is a tradition, that, long before the troops reached Lexington, an unknown horseman thundered at the door of Capt. Joseph Robbins, in Acton, waking every man and woman, and the babe in the cradle, shouting that the regulars were marching to Concord, and that the rendezvous was the old North Bridge. Capt. Robbins's son, a boy of ten years, heard the summons in the garret where he lay, and in a few minutes was on his father's old mare, a young Paul Revere, galloping along the road to rouse Capt. Isaac Davis, who commanded the minute-men of Acton. He was a young man of thirty, a gunsmith by trade, brave and thoughtful, and tenderly fond of his wife and four children. The company assembled at his shop, formed, and marched a little way, when he halted them, and returned for a moment to his house. He said to his wife, "Take good care of the children," kissed her, turned to his men, gave the order to march, and saw his home no more. Such was the history of that night in how many homes! The hearts of those men and women of Middlesex might break; but they could not waver. They had counted the cost. They knew what and whom they served; and, as the midnight summons came, they started up, and answered, "Here am I!"

Meanwhile the British bayonets, glistening in the moon, moved steadily along the road. Col. Smith heard and saw that the country was aroused, and sent back to Boston for re-enforcements, ordering Major Pitcairn, with six companies, to hasten forward, and seize the bridges at Concord. Paul Revere and Dawes had reached Lexington by midnight, and had given the alarm. The men of Lexington instantly mustered on the Green; but, as there was no sign of the enemy, they were dismissed to await his coming. He was close at hand. Pitcairn swiftly advanced, seizing every man upon the road, and was not discovered until half-past four in the morning, within a mile or two of Lexington meeting-house. Then there was a general alarm. The bell rang, drums beat, guns fired; and sixty or seventy of the Lexington militia were drawn up in line upon the Green, Capt. John Parker at their head. The British bayonets, glistening in the dawn, moved rapidly toward them. Pitcairn rode up, and angrily ordered the militia to surrender and disperse. But they held their ground. The troops fired over their heads. Still the militia stand. Then a deadly volley blazed from the British line; and eight of the Americans fell dead, and ten wounded, at the doors of their homes, and in sight of their kindred. Capt. Parker, seeing that it was massacre, not battle, ordered his men to disperse. They obeyed, some firing upon the enemy. The British troops, who had suffered little, with a loud huzza of victory pushed on toward Concord, six miles beyond.

Four hours before, Paul Revere and William Dawes had left Lexington to rouse Concord, and were soon overtaken by Dr. Samuel Prescott of that town, "a high son of liberty," who had been to Lexington upon a tender errand. A British patrol captured Revere and Dawes; but Prescott leaped a stone wall, and dashed on to Concord. Between one and two o'clock in the morning, Amos Melvin, the sentinel at the court-house, rang the bell, and roused the town. He sprang of heroic stock. One of his family, thirty years before, had commanded a company at Louisburg, and another at Crown Point; while four brothers of the same family served in the late war, and the honored names of the three who perished are carved upon your soldiers' monument. When the bell rang, the first man that appeared was William Emerson, the minister, with his gun in his hand. It was his faith that the scholar should be the minute-man of liberty, — a faith which his descendants have piously cherished, and illustrated before the world. The minute-men gathered hastily upon the Common. The citizens, hurrying from their homes, secreted the military stores. Messengers were sent to the neighboring villages, and the peaceful town prepared for battle. The minute-men of Lincoln, whose captain was William Smith, and whose lieutenant was Samuel Hoar,—a name not unknown in Middlesex, in Massachusetts, and in the country, and, wherever known, still honored for the noblest qualities of the men of the Revolution, — had joined the Concord militia and minute-men; and part of them had marched down the Lexington road to reconnoitre. Seeing the British, they fell back toward the hill, over the road at the entrance of the village, upon which stood the liberty-pole.

It was now seven o'clock. There were, perhaps, two hundred men in arms upon the hill. Below them, upon the Lexington road, a quarter of a mile away, rose a thick cloud of dust, from which, amidst proudly rolling drums, eight hundred British bayonets flashed in the morning sun. The Americans saw that battle where they stood would be mere butchery; and they fell gradually back to a rising ground about a mile north of the meeting-house, — the spot upon which we are now assembled. The British troops divided as they entered the town; the infantry coming over the hill from which the Americans had retired, the marines and grenadiers marching by the high-road. The place was well known to the British officers through their spies; and Colonel Smith, halting before the court-house, instantly sent detachments to hold the two bridges, and others to destroy the stores. But so carefully had these been secreted, that, during the two or three hours in which they were engaged in the work, the British only emptied about sixty barrels of flour, half of which was afterward saved, knocked off the trunnions of three cannon, burned sixteen new carriage-wheels and some barrels of wooden spoons and trenchers, threw five hundred pounds of balls into the pond and wells, cut down the liberty-pole, and fired the court-house.

The work was hurriedly done; for Colonel Smith, a veteran soldier, knew his peril. He had advanced twenty miles into a country of intelligent and resolute men, who were rising around him. All Middlesex was moving. From Acton and Lincoln, from Westford, Littleton, and Chelmsford, from Bedford and Billerica, from Stow, Sudbury, and Carlisle, the sons of Indian fighters, and of soldiers of the old French war, poured along the roads, shouldering the fire-locks and fowling-pieces and old king's-arms that had seen famous service when the earlier settlers had gone out against King Philip, or the later colonists had marched under the flag on which George Whitefield had written, "*Nil desperandum Cristo Duce,*' — Never despair while Christ is captain ; and those words the children of the Puritans had written on their hearts. As the minute-men from the other towns arrived, they joined the force upon the rising ground near the North Bridge, where they were drawn into line by Joseph Hosmer of Concord, who acted as adjutant. By nine o'clock, some five hundred men were assembled, and a consultation of officers and chief citizens was held. That group of Middlesex farmers, here upon Punkatasset, without thought that they were heroes, or that the day and its deeds were to be so momentous, is a group as memorable as the men of Rütli on the Swiss Alps, or the barons in the meadow of Runnymede. They confronted the mightiest empire in the world, invincible on land, supreme on the sea, whose guns had just been heard in four continents at once, girdling the globe with victory. And that empire was their mother-land, in whose renown they had shared, — the land dear to their hearts by a thousand ties of love, pride, and reverence. They took a sublime and awful responsibility. They could not know that the other colonies, or even their neighbors of Massachusetts, would justify their action. There was as yet no Declaration of Independence, no continental army. There was, indeed, a general feeling that a blow would soon be struck ; but to mistake the time, the place, the way, might be to sacrifice the great cause itself, and to ruin America. But their conscience and their judgment assured them that the hour had come. Before them lay their homes, and on the hill beyond, the graveyard in which their forefathers slept. A guard of the king's troops opposed their entrance to their own village. Those troops were at that moment searching their homes, perhaps insulting their wives and children. Already they saw the smoke as of burning houses rising in the air, and they resolved to march into the town, and to fire upon the troops if they were opposed. They resolved upon organized, aggressive, forcible resistance to the military power of Great Britain,— the first that had been offered in the colonies. All unconsciously every heart beat time to the music of the slave's epitaph in the graveyard that overhung the town : —

> "God wills us free ; man wills us slaves :
> I will as God wills : God's will be done."

Isaac Davis of Acton drew his sword, turned toward his company, and said, "I haven't a man that's afraid to go." Colonel Barrett of Concord gave the order to march. In double file, and with trailed arms, the men moved along the causeway, the Acton company in front; Major John Buttrick of Concord, Captain Isaac Davis of Acton, and Lieutenant-Colonel John Robinson of Westford, leading the way. As they approached the bridge, the British forces withdrew across it, and began to take up the planks. Major Buttrick ordered his men to hasten their march. As they came within ten or fifteen rods of the bridge, a shot was fired by the British, which wounded Jonas Brown, one of the Concord minutemen, and Luther Blanchard, fifer of the Acton company. A British volley followed; and Isaac Davis of Acton, making a way for his countrymen, like Arnold von Winkelried at Sempach, fell dead, shot through the heart. By his side fell his friend and neighbor, Abner Hosmer, a youth of twenty-two.

Seeing them fall, Major Buttrick turned to his men, and, raising his hand, cried, "Fire, fellow soldiers! for God's sake, fire!" John Buttrick gave the word. The cry rang along the line. The Americans fired. The Revolution began. It began here. Let us put off the shoes from off our feet; for the place whereon we stand is holy ground.

One of the British was killed, several were wounded; and they retreated in confusion toward the centre of the village. The engagement was doubtless seen by Smith and Pitcairn from the graveyard hill that overlooked the town; and the shots were heard by all the searching parties, which immediately returned in haste and disorder. Colonel Smith instantly prepared to retire; and at noon, one hundred years ago, at this hour, the British columns marched out of yonder square. Then and there began the retreat of British power from the American colonies. Through seven weary and wasting years it continued. From Bunker Hill to Long Island, from Princeton, Trenton, and Saratoga, from the Brandywine, Monmouth, and King's Mountain, through the bloody snow at Valley Forge, through the treachery of Arnold and of Lee, through cabals and doubt, and poverty and despair, but steadily urged by one great heart that strengthened the continent, — the heart of George Washington, — the British retreat went on from Concord Bridge and Lexington Green to the plains of Yorktown, and the king's acknowledgment of American Independence.

Of the beginning of this retreat, of that terrible march of the exhausted troops from this square to Boston, I have no time fitly to tell the tale. Almost as soon as it began, all Massachusetts was in motion. William Prescott mustered his regiment of minute-men at Pepperell; and Timothy Pickering, at Salem and Marblehead. Dedham left no man behind between the ages of sixteen and seventy. The minute-men of Worcester marched out of the town one way as the news went out the other, and, flying over the mountains, sent Berkshire to Bunker Hill. Meanwhile the men of Concord and the neighborhood, following the British over the Bridge, ran along the heights above the Lexington road, and posted themselves to await the enemy. The retreating British column, with wide-sweeping flankers, advanced steadily and slowly. No drum beat, no fife blew: there was the hushed silence of intense expectation. As the troops passed Merriam's Corner, a little beyond Concord, and the flank-guard was called in, they turned suddenly, and fired upon the Americans. The minute-men and militia instantly returned the fire; and the battle began that lasted until sunset.

When Colonel Smith ordered the retreat, although he and his officers may have had some misgivings, they had, probably, lost them in the contempt of regulars for the militia; but, from the moment of the firing at Merriam's Corner, they were undeceived. The landscape was alive with armed men. They swarmed through every wood-path and by-way, across the pastures, and over the hills. Some came up in order along the roads, as from Reading and Billerica, from East Sudbury and Bedford; and John Parker's company from Lexington waited in a woody defile to avenge the death of their comrades. The British column marched steadily on; while from trees, rocks, and fences, from houses, barns, and sheds, blazed the withering American fire. The hills echoed and flashed. The woods rang. The road became an endless ambuscade of flame. The Americans seemed to the appalled British troops to drop from the clouds, to spring from the earth. With every step, the attack was deadlier, the danger more imminent. For some time, discipline, and the plain extremity of the peril, sustained the order of the British line. But the stifling clouds of dust, the consuming thirst, the exhaustion of utter fatigue, the wagons full of wounded men moaning and dying, madly pressing through the ranks to the front, the constant falling of their comrades, officers captured and killed, and, through all, the fatal and incessant shot of an unseen foe smote with terror that haughty column, which, shrinking, bleeding, wavering, reeled through Lexington panic-stricken and broken. The officers, seeing the dire extremity, fought their way to the front, and threatened the men with death if they advanced. The breaking line recoiled a little, and even steadied under one of the sharpest attacks of the day; for not as yet were Hessians hired to enslave Americans, and it was English blood and pluck on both sides. At two o'clock in the afternoon, a half-mile beyond Lexington meeting-house, just as the English officers saw that destruction or surrender was the only alternative, Lord Percy, with a re-enforcement of twelve hundred men, came up, and, opening with two cannon upon the Americans, succored his flying and desperate comrades, who fell upon the ground among Percy's troops, their parched tongues hanging from their mouths.

The flower of General Gage's army was now upon the field; but its commander saw at once that its sole hope of safety was to continue the retreat. After half an hour's delay, the march was resumed, and with it the barbarities, as well as the sufferings, of war. Lord Percy threw out flanking-parties, which entered the houses upon the line of march, plundering and burning. The fields of Menotomy, or Arlington, through which lay the road, became a plain of blood and fire. But the American pursuit was relentless; and beyond Lexington

the lower counties and towns came hurrying to the battle.
Many a man afterward famous was conspicuous that day;
and, near West Cambridge, Joseph Warren was the inspiring
soul of the struggle. It was now past five o'clock. The
British ammunition was giving out. The officers, too much
exposed in the saddle, alighted, and marched with the men,
who, as they approached Charlestown, encountered the hot-
test fire of the day. General Gage had learned the perilous
extremity of his army from a messenger sent by Percy, and
had issued a proclamation threatening to lay Charlestown in
ashes if the troops were attacked in the streets. The town
hummed with the vague and appalling rumors of the events
of the day, and, just before sunset, the excited inhabitants
heard the distant guns, and soon saw the British troops running along the old Cambridge road to Charlestown Neck,
firing as they came. They had just escaped the militia
seven hundred strong from Salem and Marblehead, — the
flower of Essex; and, as the sun was setting, they entered
Charlestown and gained the shelter of their frigate-guns.
Then General Heath ordered the American pursuit to stop,
and the battle was over. But all that day and night the news
was flying from mouth to mouth, from heart to heart, rousing
every city, town, and solitary farm in the colonies; and before
the last shot of the minute-men on the British retreat from
Concord Bridge was fired, or the last wounded grenadier had
been rowed across the river, the whole country was in arms.
Massachusetts, New England, America, were closing around
the city; and the siege of Boston, and the war of American
Independence, had begun.

Such was the opening battle of the Revolution, — a conflict, which, so far as we can see, saved civil liberty in two
hemispheres, — saved England as well as America, and

whose magnificent results shine through the world as the beacon-light of free popular government. And who won this victory? The minute-men and militia, who, in the history of our English race, have been always the vanguard of freedom. The minute-man of the American Revolution — who was he? He was the husband and father, who, bred to love liberty, and to know that lawful liberty is the sole guaranty of peace and progress, left the plough in the furrow, and the hammer on the bench, and, kissing wife and children, marched to die — or to be free. He was the son and lover, the plain, shy youth of the singing-school and the village choir, whose heart beat to arms for his country, and who felt, though he could not say, with the old English cavalier, —

> "I could not love thee, deare, so much,
> Loved I not honor more."

The minute-man of the Revolution! — he was the old, the middle-aged, and the young. He was Captain Miles of Concord, who said that he went to battle as he went to church. He was Captain Davis of Acton, who reproved his men for jesting on the march. He was Deacon Josiah Haynes of Sudbury, eighty years old, who marched with his company to the South Bridge at Concord, then joined in the hot pursuit to Lexington, and fell as gloriously as Warren at Bunker Hill. He was James Hayward of Acton, twenty-two years old, foremost in that deadly race from Concord to Charlestown, who raised his piece at the same moment with a British soldier, each exclaiming, "You are a dead man!" The Briton dropped, shot through the heart. James Hayward fell mortally wounded. "Father," he said, "I started with forty balls: I have three left. I never did such a day's work before. Tell mother not to mourn too much; and tell her whom I love more than my mother, that I am not sorry I turned out."

This was the minute-man of the Revolution, the rural citizen trained in the common school, the church, and the town meeting, who carried a bayonet that thought, and whose gun, loaded with a principle, brought down not a man, but a system. Him we gratefully recall to-day, — him, in yon manly figure wrought in the metal which but feebly typifies his inexorable will, we commit in his immortal youth to the reverence of our children. And here among these peaceful fields, — here in the county whose children first gave their blood for American union and independence, and, eighty-six years later, gave it first also for a truer union and a larger liberty, — here in the heart of Middlesex, county of Lexington and Concord and Bunker Hill, stand fast, Son of Liberty, as the minute-man stood at the old North Bridge! But should we or our descendants, false to liberty, false to justice and humanity, betray in any way their cause, spring into life as a hundred years ago, take one more step, descend, and lead us, as God led you in saving America, to save the hopes of man!

At the end of a century, we can see the work of this day as our fathers could not: we can see that then the final movement began of a process long and unconsciously preparing, which was to intrust liberty to new forms and institutions that seemed full of happy promise for mankind. And now, for nearly a century, what was formerly called the experiment of a representative republic of imperial extent and power has been tried. Has it fulfilled the hopes of its founders, and the just expectations of mankind? I have already glanced at its early and fortunate conditions, and we know how vast and splendid were its early growth and development. Our material statistics soon dazzled the world. Europe no longer sneered, but gazed in wonder, waiting and watching. Our population doubled every fifteen years; and our wealth every ten years. Every little stream among the hills turned a mill; and the great inland seas, bound by the genius of Clinton to the ocean, became the highway of boundless commerce, the path of unprecedented empire. Our farms were the granary of other lands. Our cotton-fields made England rich. Still we chased the whale in the Pacific Ocean, and took fish in the tumbling seas of Labrador. We hung out friendly lights along thousands of miles of coast to tempt the trade of every clime; and wherever, on the dim rim of the globe, there was a harbor, it was white with American sails. Meanwhile at home the political foreboding of Federalism had died away; and its very wail seemed a tribute to the pacific glories of the land.

> "The ornament of beauty is Suspect,
> A crow that flies in heaven's sweetest air."

The government was felt to be but a hand of protection and blessing; labor was fully employed; capital was secure; the army was a jest; enterprise was pushing through the Alleghanies, grasping and settling the El Dorado of the prairies, and still braving the wilderness, reached out toward the Rocky Mountains, and, reversing the voyages of Columbus, rediscovered the Old World from the New. America was the Benjamin of nations, the best-beloved of Heaven; and the starry flag of the United States flashed a line of celestial light around the world, the harbinger of freedom, peace, and prosperity.

Such was the vision and the exulting faith of fifty years ago. "Atlantis hath risen from the ocean!" cried

Edward Everett to applauding Harvard; and Daniel Webster answered from Bunker Hill, "If we fail, popular governments are impossible." So far as they could see, they stood among the unchanged conditions of the early republic. And those conditions are familiar. The men who founded the republic were few in number, planted chiefly along a temperate coast, remote from the world. They were a homogeneous people, increasing by their own multiplication, speaking the same language, of the same general religious faith, cherishing the same historic and political traditions, universally educated, hardy, thrifty, with general equality of fortune, and long and intelligent practice of self-government, while the slavery that existed among them, inhuman in itself, was not seriously defended, and was believed to be disappearing. But within the last half-century causes then latent, or wholly incalculable before, have radically changed those conditions; and we enter upon the second century of the republic with responsibilities which neither our fathers, nor the men of fifty years ago, could possibly foresee.

Think, for instance, of the change wrought by foreign immigration, with all its necessary consequences. In the State of Massachusetts to-day, the number of citizens of foreign birth who have no traditional association with the story of Concord and Lexington is larger than the entire population of the State on the day of battle. The first fifty years after that day brought to the whole country fewer immigrants than are now living in Massachusetts alone. At the end of that half-century, when Mr. Everett stood here, less than three hundred thousand foreign immigrants had come to this country; but, in the fifty years that have since elapsed, there has been an immigration of more than nine millions of persons. The aggregate population in the last fifty years has advanced somewhat more than threefold; the foreign immigration, more than thirty-fold; so that now immigrants and the children of immigrants are a quarter of the whole population. This enormous influx of foreigners has added an immense ignorance, and entire unfamiliarity with republican ideas and habits, to the voting-class. It has brought other political traditions, other languages, and other religious faiths. It has introduced powerful and organized influences not friendly to the republican principle of freedom of thought and action. It is to the change produced by immigration that we owe the first serious questioning of the public school system, which was the nursery of the early republic, and which is to-day the palladium of free popular government.

Do not misunderstand me. I am not lamenting, even in thought, the boundless hospitality of America. I do not forget that the whole European race came hither but yesterday, and has been domesticated here not yet three hundred years. I am not insensible of the proud claim of America to be the refuge of the oppressed of every clime; nor do I doubt in her maturity her power, if duly directed, to assimilate whole nations, if need be, as in her infancy she achieved her independence, and in her prime maintained her unity. But if she has been the hope of the world, and is so still, it is because she has understood both the conditions and the perils of freedom, and watches carefully the changing conditions under which republican liberty is to be maintained. She will still welcome to her ample bosom all who choose to be called her children. But, if she is to remain the mother of liberty, it will not be the result of those craven counsels whose type is the ostrich burying his head in the sand, but of that wise and heroic statesmanship, whose symbol is her own heaven-soaring eagle, gazing undazzled even at the spots upon the sun.

Again: within the century, steam has enormously expanded the national domain; and every added mile is an added strain to our system. The marvellous ease of communication both by rail and telegraph tends to obliterate conservative local lines, and to make a fatal centralization more possible. The telegraph, which instantly echoes the central command at the remotest point, becomes both a facility and a temptation to exercise command; while below upon the rail the armed blow swiftly follows the word that flies along the wire. Steam concentrates population in cities. But, when the government was formed, the people were strictly rural, and there were but six cities with eight thousand inhabitants or more. In 1790, only one-thirtieth of the population lived in cities: in 1870, more than one-fifth. Steam destroys the natural difficulties of communication; but those very difficulties are barriers against invasion, and protect the independence of each little community, the true foundation of our free republican system. In New England, the characteristic village and local life of the last century perishes in the age of steam. Meanwhile the enormous accumulation of capital engaged in great enterprises, with unscrupulous greed of power, constantly tends to make itself felt in corruption of the press, which moulds public opinion, and of the legislature which makes the laws. Thus steam and the telegraph tend to the concentration of capital, and the consolidation of political power, — a tendency which threatens liberty, and which was wholly unknown when the republic began, and was unsuspected fifty years ago. Sweet liberty is a mountain nymph, because mountains baffle the pursuer. But the inventions that level mountains and annihilate space alarm that gracious spirit, who sees her greater insecurity. But stay, heaven-eyed maid, and stay forever! Behold, our devoted wills shall be thy invincible Alps, our loyal hearts thy secret bower, the spirit of our fathers a cliff of adamant, that engineering skill can never pierce nor any foe can scale.

But the most formidable problem for popular government which the opening of our second century presents springs from a source which was unsuspected a hundred years ago, and which the orators of fifty years since forbore to name. This was the system of slave labor, which vanished in civil war. But slavery had not been the fatal evil that it was, if, with its abolition, its consequences had disappeared. It holds us still in mortmain. Its dead hand is strong as its living power was terrible. Emancipation has left the republic exposed to a new and extraordinary trial of the principles and practices of free government. A civilization resting upon slavery, as formerly in part of the country, however polished and ornate, is necessarily aristocratic, and hostile to republican equality, while the exigencies of such a society forbid that universal education which is indispensable to wise popular government. When war emancipates the slaves and makes them equal citizens, the ignorance and venality which are the fatal legacies of slavery to the subject class, whether white or black, and the natural alienation of the master class, which alone has political knowledge and experience, with all the secret conspiracies, the reckless corruption, the political knavery, springing naturally from such a situation, and ending often in menacing disorder that seems to invite the military interference and supervision of the government — all this accumulation of difficulty and danger lays a strain along the very fibre of free institutions; for it suggests the twofold question, whether the vast addition of the ignorance of the emancipated vote to that of the immigrant vote may not overwhelm the intelligent vote of the country, and whether the constant appeal to the central hand of power — however necessary it may seem, and for whatever reason of humanity and justice it may be urged — must not necessarily destroy that local self-reliance which was the very seed of the American republic, and fatally familiarize the country with that employment of military power which is inconsistent with free institutions, and bold resistance to which has forever consecrated the spot on which we stand.

These are some of the more obvious changes in the conditions under which the republic is to be maintained. I mention them merely; but every wise patriot sees and ponders them. Does he therefore despond? Heaven forbid! When was there ever an auspicious day for humanity that was not one of doubt and conflict? The robust moral manhood of America confronts the future with steadfast faith and indomitable will, raising the old battle-cry of the race for larger liberty and surer law. It sees clouds, indeed, as Sam Adams saw them when this day dawned; but with him it sees through and through them, and with him thanks God for the glorious morning. There is, indeed, a fashion of scepticism of American principles, even among some Americans; but it is one of the oldest and worst fashions in our history. There is a despondency, which fondly fancies, that, in its beginning, the American republic moved proudly toward the future with all the splendid assurance of the Persian Xerxes descending on the shores of Greece, but that it sits to-day among shattered hopes, like Xerxes above his ships at Salamis. And when was this golden age? Was it when John Adams appealed from the baseness of his own time to the greater candor and patriotism of this? Was it when Fisher Ames mourned over lost America, like Rachel for her children, and would not be comforted? Was it when William

Wirt said that he sought in vain for a man fit for the presidency or for great responsibility? Was it when Chancellor Livingston saw only a threatening future, because Congress was so feeble? Was it when we ourselves saw the industry, the commerce, the society, the church, the courts, the statesmanship, the conscience, of America seemingly prostrate under the foot of slavery? Was this the golden age of these doubting sighs, this the region behind the north wind of these reproachful regrets? And is it the young nation which with prayer and faith, with untiring devotion and unconquerable will, has lifted its bruised and broken body from beneath that crushing heel, whose future is distrusted?

Nay, this very scepticism is one of the foes that we must meet and conquer. Remember, fellow-citizens, that the impulse of republican government given a century ago at the old North Bridge has shaken every government in the world, but has been itself wholly unshaken by them. It has made monarchy impossible in France. It has freed the Russian serfs. It has united Germany against ecclesiastical despotism. It has flashed into the night of Spain. It has emancipated Italy, and discrowned the pope as king. In England, repealing the disabilities of Catholic and Hebrew, it forecasts the separation of Church and State, and step by step transforms monarchy into another form of republic. And here at home how glorious its story! In a tremendous war between men of the same blood, — men who recognize and respect each other's valor, — we have proved what was always doubted, — the prodigious power, endurance, and resources of a republic; and, in emancipating an eighth of the population, we have at last gained the full opportunity of the republican principle. Sir, it is the signal felicity of this occasion, that, on the one hundredth anniversary of the first battle in the war of American Independence, I may salute you, who led to victory the citizen-soldiers of American liberty, as the first elected president of the free republic of the United States. Fortunate man! to whom God has given the priceless boon of associating your name with that triumph of freedom which will presently bind the East and the West, the North and the South, in a closer and more perfect union for the establishment of justice, and the security of the blessings of liberty, than these States have ever known.

Fellow-citizens, that union is the lofty task which this hallowed day and this sacred spot impose upon us. And what cloud of doubt so dark hangs over us as that which lowered above the colonies when the troops of the king marched into this town, and the men of Middlesex resolved to pass the Bridge? With their faith and their will we shall win their victory. No royal governor, indeed, sits in yon stately capital, no hostile fleet for many a year has vexed the waters of our coasts, nor is any army but our own ever likely to tread our soil. Not such are our enemies to-day. They do not come proudly stepping to the drum-beat, with bayonets flashing in the morning sun. But wherever party spirit shall strain the ancient guaranties of freedom; or bigotry and ignorance shall lay their fatal hands upon education; or the arrogance of caste shall strike at equal rights; or corruption shall poison the very springs of national life, — there, minute-men of liberty, are your Lexington Green and Concord Bridge; and as you love your country and your kind, and would have your children rise up and call you blessed, spare not the enemy! Over the hills, out of the earth, down from the clouds, pour in resistless might. Fire from every rock and tree, from door and window, from hearthstone and chamber; hang upon his flank and rear from noon to sunset, and so, through a land blazing with holy indignation, hurl the hordes of ignorance and corruption and injustice back, back, in utter defeat and ruin.

At ten minutes before one o'clock, before the close of the oration, Mr. Curtis paused at the request of Judge Hoar, who said, —

"Ladies and gentlemen, Concord always keeps faith with Lexington. We promised to deliver to them the President at one o'clock; and he is therefore obliged to leave. Give him three parting cheers."

Three cheers were then given, which the President acknowledged by bowing to the assembly, and with the Vice-President, the Cabinet, Governor Gaston, the Executive Council and Legislature of Massachusetts, the Judges of the Supreme Judicial Court, and several others of our guests who had accepted the Lexington invitation, left the tent.

A special train had been provided to convey this distinguished party over the Middlesex Central Railroad to Lexington; but the road was hopelessly blocked; and the Committee, in order that all the exercises, whether in Concord or Lexington, might be carried out as far as it was in their power to forward them, tendered carriages to the President and his Cabinet, and to Governor Gaston and the Executive Council. This courtesy was accepted by General Grant, who, with his Cabinet, was rapidly driven over the road to Lexington, and by this means arrived there in season to review the procession, and attend the dinner. Governor Gaston, however, who, with the First Corps of Cadets and the Legislature, was waiting at the dépôt for the stipulated train, felt obliged to decline our offer of transportation, as he did not wish to leave his escort behind. After a delay of somewhat over an hour, the blockade was so far broken as to allow one train to pass over the road, carrying those who were anxiously waited for to participate in the afternoon exercises in Lexington.

At the conclusion of the oration, the Fifth Regiment M. V. M. was drawn up in two lines, extending from the platform entrance of the oration tent to the east entrance of the dinner tent; and through the lane thus formed, the invited guests were immediately conducted to dinner. At the same time, the grand entrance on the west was opened, and the general public admitted.

EXERCISES IN THE DINNER TENT.

EXERCISES IN THE DINNER TENT.

The dinner tent was a magnificent sight. Of new, snowy canvas, four hundred and ten feet in length, eighty-five feet wide, and forty feet in height, surmounted with flags, it was the centre of attraction. It was owned by Andrew Erickson of Boston, who deserves the greatest credit for his skill in spreading so large a canvas, and protecting it from the high winds that had prevailed for several days.

The interior was profusely decorated with flags, bunting, and streamers. Long pennants were festooned from the top of each pole to the base of the canopy. On the thirteen tent-poles were hung as many shields bearing the coats-of-arms of the thirteen original states, and underneath each shield two American flags were gracefully looped. The following mottoes in conspicuous letters were hung on the sides of the canvas: —

"*Concordia res parvæ crescunt.*"

"Concord that elevates the mind and stills." — WORDSWORTH.

"'Tis still observed those men most valiant are,
That are most modest ere they come to war." — HERRICK.

"The first shot fired in America separates the Colonies." — CHATHAM.

"They little thought how pure a light
   With years should gather round that day,
How love should keep their memories bright,
   How wide a realm their sons would sway." — BRYANT.

"We find in our dull road their shining track." — LOWELL.

"Not unto us, O Lord, not unto us, but unto thy name, give glory."

"So nigh is grandeur to our dust,
   So near is God to man,
When Duty whispers low, 'Thou must,'
   The youth replies, 'I can.'" — EMERSON.

Tables to accommodate four thousand persons were placed in rows running across the tent from side to side. On the south-easterly side, a platform was arranged, the floor of which was on the level of the ground tables. On this platform were placed tables to accommodate two hundred persons. At the centre table were seated the President of the Day, the Orator of the Day, Mr. Ralph Waldo Emerson, Hon. James G. Blaine, and Hon. Joseph R. Hawley; on the right, Governor Ingersoll of Connecticut and his staff, Governor Dingley of Maine and his staff, and Governor Peck of Vermont and his staff; on the left, Hon. George S. Boutwell, Hon. George F. Hoar, President Eliot of Harvard College, and other distinguished guests. The tables at both ends of the tent were filled by the veteran military companies, and by the Fifth Regiment M. V. M. The whole centre was filled by a great concourse of ladies and gentlemen. In front of the table of the President of the Day was placed a collection of relics, among which were, —

The sword of Captain Isaac Davis, carried by him at the old North Bridge.

The musket of Major John Buttrick, fired by him in answer to his famous order, "Fire, fellow-soldiers! for God's sake, fire!"

A sword taken by Nathaniel Bemis of Watertown from a British officer whom he shot; and the gun, marked "David Bemis, 1775," with which he shot him.

The sword of Lieutenant Davis of Bedford, worn by him at the North Bridge.

The sword of Oliver Wheeler of Acton, worn by him April 19, 1775.

A six-pound cannon-ball, thrown into the mill-pond by the British, and found long afterwards.

The sword of Lieutenant James Potter of the British marines, who was taken prisoner April 19, 1775, and confined in the house of Reuben Brown. This sword bears the inscription, "X$^{th.}$ Rgt. Co. VI. N$^o.$ 10."

A British cartridge-box, stamped "G. R.," taken from the regulars.

A powder horn, inscribed "Concord, William Buttrick. His Horn, Sept. 15, 1774."

The powder-horn of Amos Barrett.

The sword of Captain Nathan Barrett, carried by him April 19, 1775.

A powder-horn carried by Joseph Chaffin of Acton, at Concord, and during the chase to Charlestown Neck, and at Bunker Hill.

A stack of Revolutionary flint-lock muskets.

The old flag carried by the Bedford minute-men, mentioned above in the account of the procession.

One of the famous "Coffin handbills," styled "The Bloody Butchery by the British troops, or the Runaway Fight of the Regulars,"
and various other interesting relics of the fight.

After somewhat more than half an hour had been spent in dining, the American Band of Providence played Auld Lang Syne, and a medley of patriotic airs. The President of the Day then rose, called the assemblage to order, and said, —

FELLOW-CITIZENS, — Patriotic memories are the strength of a nation. America, as a nation, to-day enters upon her second century. We have assembled to celebrate as worthily as we may the great centennial anniversary of the Revolution. The British parliament in 1774 had voted a law to prohibit the holding of town meetings in New England, except for the purpose of choosing officers. It was too late: the town meetings had done their work. The villages of New England had responded to Faneuil Hall; the discussions in the towns had responded to the fiery eloquence of Adams and Otis; preparations had been made; the people had determined to maintain their liberties at any cost; and they were waiting only for the time when by any forcible act by which their property should be seized, or their rights violated, they might be called upon to defend both in arms. And the day came, — a glorious day for Lexington, for Concord, for Acton, for the towns of Middlesex and Essex and Norfolk, for Massachusetts, and for the country. It was accidental only, that the spark first kindled here into a flame; for the whole country, from one end to the other, was heated, and ready to flame at the slightest spark. And when the day came — have you considered, fellow-citizens, what a day of transformation it was? The men who were called from their beds at midnight, at the tap of the drum at Lexington, were English colonists. The men who marched down to the old North Bridge, saying that they had a right to go to Concord on the King's highway, and they would go to Concord, were British subjects, claiming the rights of Englishmen. That was America on the morning of the 19th of April, 1775. At night on that day, the American people were besieging in Boston a foreign enemy, whom they had driven in hurried and ignominious rout to take refuge under the shelter of his ships-of-war. The American nation was born that day. Every thing that succeeded it in the Revolution was but a corollary of this first and primal proposition. At Philadelphia, in 1776, our fathers declared what had already been made a fixed fact. All the victories of the war were simply the steps by which the American people were driving the

British Government to an acknowledgment of the fact, which was established as surely on the 19th of April, 1775, as it is established on the 19th of April, 1875. When a people have found something that they are willing to die for; when the humblest men among them, who could have gone on tilling their fields, working at their trades, and taking their comfort and ease in life, are willing instead, for a principle, for a public object, as citizens who feel that they have a duty to mankind and their country to discharge, to take their lives in their hands, and say, "We will lay them down, if need be, for this object," you have before you a people whose independence is secure, whose future is certain.

I do not propose to detain you to listen to any speech of mine. The nineteenth of April, I believe, pervades me through and through, and I could talk about it for a week; but I do not intend to do so. I know it is in all of you also. Every one of you feels it as thoroughly, — the spirit of the Revolution. I offer as the first regular sentiment of the day: —

The Nineteenth of April, Seventeen Hundred and Seventy-five: A glorious day for Lexington and Concord, for the towns of Middlesex, for Massachusetts, for America, for freedom, and the rights of mankind. "Every blow struck for liberty among men since the 19th of April, 1775, has but echoed the guns of that eventful morning."

The President: The President of the United States has left us to unite in the kindred ceremonies at Lexington; but we have the pleasure to have with us a gentleman whom I shall invite to address you, in whom, I may say, Pennsylvania has undertaken to pay back the debt which she owes to New England for giving her Benjamin Franklin, — a man whose national fame, and right to speak for the people of the United States, need no introduction and no comment from me, — James G. Blaine.

Mr. Blaine was received with loud applause as he rose to respond.

REMARKS OF HON. JAMES G. BLAINE.

MY modesty will not permit me to accept the reason given by the honored Chairman of the Day for calling me out as the first speaker. It occurs to me that he was unconsciously moved by an entirely different consideration. He has served recently in the House of Representatives, where he learned, that, on a call of States, Maine always stands first; and, owing to that habit, I have the great honor of being presented to you. In listening, this morning,

to the matchless eulogy of a matchless event in history, I was struck by one
fact which the gravity of the occasion forbade the eloquent orator from
alluding to. They have been searching these hundred years past for reasons
why the first blow for American liberty should have been struck at Concord;
but I think they have neglected the real, primal, instinctive reason that
underlay the whole. The truth is, that the people of Concord from the early
settlement of the town had been, to use a somewhat slang phrase, "spoiling
for a fight." They had the Apostle Eliot among them early to train and
subdue the Indians; but they relied a great deal more upon their muskets
than upon his mild maxims. When the colonists got into a row with Sir
Edmund Andros, it was a company from Concord that drove him away;
when King Philip attempted his ravages, it was Concord men that met
him; and, when the period of the Revolution came, it was just as inevitable
that the first conflict should come at Concord, as it was that King George
should insist upon the measures that should drive the colonists to resistance.
I have, therefore, had no trouble in determining in my own mind, from the
fighting generations of Concord people that I have myself known, that here
was the precise place where the clash of arms should first resound. In
reading the annals of the great event that we have been celebrating to-day,
you will find that one of the first things the people of Concord did was to
refuse to allow the royal judges to sit; and, further, that they humbled the
Tories. Lord, how I pity those Tories! I believe the name of a single Tory
that was humbled by the Concord people has never been recorded in history.
They never could find out where they went; but it is perfectly easy to believe, that, under the weight of the humiliation inflicted through the Concord
indignation, every one resorted to the better fate of suicide.

We have been told by an eminent English historian that there were fifteen decisive battles in the world. He closed his history about 1854. I think, if he had
written a little while later, he would have found a few more decisive struggles
to add to the list. In going over those battles, from Marathon to Waterloo,
you get, in effect, the history of all the great powers that have risen and have
fallen, — the Persian, the Assyrian, the Egyptian, the Roman, and the Greek.
The great changes that have come over the face of modern Europe are also
chronicled. But there is one list of battles that has not yet been gathered
by the historian. We are all familiar with Marathon; we all know what
Waterloo did; we know, also, what was done at Sedan; we know what was
done on our own continent, at Petersburg, in the Wilderness, at Vicksburg
and Chattanooga; but that list of battles which, I may say, may be classed as
those that *force the issue*, whether in the moral, or political, or military world,
have never yet been classified. John Quincy Adams fought one in the
House of Representatives, when he insisted upon presenting a petition for a
slave. That forced the issue, and was the battle which decided the right of
petition in this country. A Pennsylvania representative (I speak of it with
some sensibility, since my honored friend alluded to myself somewhat in that

connection) forced the great issue of slavery in this country, by moving a proviso to a simple territorial bill. And what these Concord men did was simply to force the issue. It was a small battle. The men killed in the first fight — and, indeed, in the whole day's transactions, bloody as they were — would not amount to the loss in a picket skirmish in the last war; but yet, it gave birth to what? To a nation, and a nation so vast and so grand, that, if I were to stop to survey what has since transpired, I should want more than the week Judge Hoar desired, to rid himself of the impression of the 19th of April. Why, we were but three millions of people then. The House of Representatives, which I have had the honor to serve in for some years, has to-day more than two thirds of its members taken from the country where the foot of the white man, up to that day, had never trodden except the adventurous hunter. More than two thirds of the entire House of Representatives come from land then undreamed of for settlement. The day that gun was fired across yonder bridge there did not exist on the American continent fifty thousand white settlers fifty miles from the tide-water of the Atlantic. It was only a narrow rim of people, stretching from Maine to Georgia, but not penetrating the interior at all. But all this has followed, as directly as consequence follows cause, from the blow that was struck that day in the small fight at Concord Bridge.

Gentlemen, to allude to that battle, or even to gather up a single crumb from the table at which we have fed so bounteously to-day, seems to be a work of supererogation, if not of impossibility. All that remains to us, all that can remain to us, is to see, that, one hundred years hence, we may be remembered as honorably and as indelibly as those whose deeds we this day celebrate. It might possibly have been a matter of doubt with us, but for the late terrible experience of this country, whether we had within us the same heroic blood that fought and fell that day. But happily, out of the great griefs and the great sufferings of our own time, we know that we, their descendants, have not grown less strong in arm or less dauntless in heart than those that fought for us then. It remains for us to transmit to those who come after us a record in the line of civil duty, in the line of preserving all for which that generation and our own have fought, that shall secure to our descendants, to the remotest generations, the blessings which nothing but public virtue and personal courage can give to any people.

Music: "America" and "Yankee Doodle."

The President: I propose to present matters on this occasion in a somewhat orderly and methodical manner, and I call to mind that we are honored by the presence to-day of a representative of the blood of Paul Revere; and that memory, as you all know, belongs to the night before, and very early in the morning before, the events either at Lexington or Concord; and I give you as a sentiment, —

Paul Revere's Ride.

> "A hurry of hoofs in the village street,
> A shape in the moonlight, a bulk in the dark,
> And beneath from the pebbles, in passing, a spark
> Struck out by a steed flying fearless and fleet;
> That was all. And yet through the gloom and the light
> The fate of a nation was riding that night;
> And the spark struck out by that steed in his flight
> Kindled the land into flame with its heat."

I ask the grandson of Paul Revere to stand up, and let us see him. He does not make speeches any more than his grandfather did. His name is JOHN REVERE.

Upon Mr. Revere's manifesting himself to the assembly, he was greeted with three hearty cheers.

The President: First of those who fell, in our memory of the day we celebrate, are the martyrs on Lexington Common. Their deeds, their immortal fame, are now being worthily celebrated by their neighbors and descendants at Lexington. I give you: —

The martyrs on Lexington Common, — Parker, Monroe, Hadley, the Harringtons, Muzzey, Brown.

> "With us their names shall live
> Through long succeeding years,
> Embalmed with all our hearts can give,
> Our praises, and our tears."

FELLOW-CITIZENS, — No one from Lexington can be found here to-day to respond to this sentiment, as I suppose no one from Concord could be found at Lexington to acknowledge any courtesies extended to us. So be it. The legacy of glory will go round, and is enough for all. But I thought it fitting to send, and have sent, in your name, a message to Lexington from Concord, to this effect: —

"Concord sends greeting to Lexington on the hundredth anniversary of the glorious morning, by the hands of the President of the United States. The Great Republic, whose thirty-seven states span the continent from ocean to ocean, is the harvest of which the seed was sown on the 19th of April, 1775."

Music.

The President: And next in memory are the men who were first to fall at the North Bridge at Concord, —

Captain Isaac Davis, and Abner Hosmer, a private of his company of Minute-Men of Acton, the first to lay down their lives in an organized military attack upon the soldiers of Great Britain in the Revolutionary War. The grateful country for whose liberties they died accords to them a foremost place upon her roll of honor.

I invite the Rev. Mr. Wood of Acton to respond on behalf of that town.

ADDRESS OF REV. F. P. WOOD.

I FULLY appreciate the honor done me on this memorable occasion in being permitted, in the name of the town of Acton, to respond to this toast. But without wasting words, when time is most precious, who were the men whose names appear in the toast just presented? No better reply can be given than that which is found in this sentiment. They were citizen-soldiers of Acton, and Provincial minute-men, who, one hundred years ago to-day, demonstrated the quality of their patriotism by being the first to lay down their lives in a regularly organized defence of their country in its just rights against the encroachments of Great Britain. The Orator of the Day has done such ample justice to the causes which led to the Revolution, which had its real beginning one hundred years ago, that to add to it would be superfluous.

I will simply say, it is very evident that the town of Acton was alive to the importance of passing events, from the fact, that in 1770, and again in 1772, her citizens, in town meeting assembled, passed most emphatic resolutions in remonstrance to the oppressive policy of the British ministry. That the town of Acton was, at least, abreast of the patriotic sentiment of the time is also proven by the fact, that, one hundred years ago to-day, she had three military companies thoroughly drilled, ready for immediate action, — drilled, too, at the expense of the town, though the town was then poor in every thing but patriotism. In these companies there were enrolled nearly one hundred and fifty men, though the population of the town was but little over half a thousand. In those days, every one in Acton who was able to carry a gun was a soldier, and, before the day was over, had a part in the achievements which are to-day celebrated. ‘One of these companies was a choice one of minute-men, under the command of Captain Isaac Davis, a fit leader for such a company of men, — courageous and beloved. He was in the flush of early manhood, being only thirty years old, though the father of four children, all of whom were sick on the morning of the eventful day. Abner Hosmer, a young man of twenty-three, and son of a revered deacon in the Congregational church, was a member of Davis's company. In accord with the recommendation of the Provincial Congress, the Acton companies had drilled regularly during the previous winter and spring. It is, probably, the case, however, that very few of them thought that a tilt of arms with the troops of King George was really imminent. But one hundred years ago this morning, before dawn, hours before the British entered Concord, a horseman, whose name was never known, rode at full speed up to the house of Captain Robbins, the commander of a militia company, the commissioned officer of Acton, who lived nearest the North Bridge, and with a heavy club, as it seemed to those within, struck the corner of the house, and cried at the top of his voice, "Captain Robbins! Captain Robbins! Up, up! The regulars have come to Concord. Quick as possible alarm Acton!" In a very few minutes the son of Captain Robbins, a mere lad, was on horseback, and hastening to the house of Captain Davis, who commanded the minute-men, with the thrilling message so mysteriously given; and he, though his children were sick, in an incredibly short time had his company together, ready for the march to Concord. Time does not permit me even to refer to what took place as the brave leader and his men set forth upon their perilous march. I will only say that his whole manner, as he went forth, carried a presentiment that he should never return alive. At this point allow me to quote the words of a poet who has attempted to portray the scene in verse : —

> "Then on the children of this man the flames
> Of fever fed, wasting their feeble frames.
> His wife was worn with watching o'er their bed.
> 'And must thou leave these children thus?' she said.
> 'But we've a Guardian : I'll not stop thee, no!
> Thy country calls thee : God is with thee, go!'
> 'Guard well these children!' is his brief reply,
> A tear-drop standing in the father's eye ;
> When Acton's minute-men to Concord sped
> In martial order, Davis at their head."

So energetically did Captain Davis enter into the spirit of his work, and so promptly did his men respond to his call, that, at nine o'clock on the morning of this glorious day, he had his company marshalled in line of battle with the Provincial troops near the old North Bridge.

Here let me quote a part of the inscription upon the stately monument which stands near my home on Acton Common, over the ashes of the three citizens of Acton who fell mortally wounded one hundred years ago to-day.

This monument was erected by the State of Massachusetts and the town of Acton as a tribute to the memory of these heroic men.

In the inscription upon this monument appear these words : —

On the morning of that eventful day, the provincial officers held a council of war near the old North Bridge in Concord; and as they separated Davis exclaimed, "I haven't a man that is afraid to go!" and immediately marched his company from the left to the right of the line, and led in the first organized attack upon the troops of George III., in that memorable war, which, by the help of God, made the thirteen colonies independent of Great Britain, and gave political being to the United States of America.

I quote these words especially as an authorized encomium upon the services of Captain Davis.

I am happy that to-day there is present on this occasion the son of one of Captain Davis's company, who proved without a doubt that his father's patriot blood still flows in his veins, by going through Baltimore with the Acton company, under the lead of Captain Daniel Tuttle, in the glorious Old Sixth Regiment, which, in that baptism of blood, covered itself with glory on the 19th of April, 1861, no less than did their fathers on the 19th of April, 1775. Truly the soul of Captain Davis was marching on in this goodly company of Acton. This man before mentioned, — Mr. Luke Smith, — whose father fought at the old North Bridge, has gone over the ground about this sacred spot with his father, and heard from his lips the thrilling story which is told in a few words upon the monument.

I would be the last to detract from the courage of any of those who were engaged in the movement in which the Acton men held the post of danger. They were all of them men of stout hearts, lineal descendants of Puritans, who, when in the way of duty, like John Knox, "feared not the face of man." Others will recount their praises: to me it is given to speak simply for the men of Acton. Captain Davis was the youngest commander of minute-men. As men advance in years, they become more cautious. For the very reason that Davis was the youngest captain, and had a company of picked men, it might be expected, without disparaging the courage of any one, that he would speak first as a volunteer, with his men, to take the post of greatest danger.

The orator of the day has portrayed to us what it was to lead in the attack one hundred years ago this morning. It was to take a step, which, though long talked of and threatened, had not really yet been taken. It was to cease to be mere remonstrants, and to become rebels. It was to expose themselves, not simply to the perils of battle, but to the ignominy of the scaffold. Major Buttrick, Captain Davis, Colonel Robinson, and the Acton minute-men, led the column of Provincial soldiers as they took this position. At the first fire from the enemy, the fifer of the Acton company was wounded; and at the first volley, Captain Davis, in the act of raising his gun to take aim, was shot, and instantly killed. His blood gushed out in one great stream: it drenched his clothes, and these shoe-buckles which I hold in my hand, and fell as a baptism of patriotism upon some of the comrades who stood near. Abner Hosmer, a member of his company, fell at the same volley. But these men did not die in vain. No, no! The mantle of their patriotism fell upon their fellow-soldiers; and, before the sun went down, the arrogant servants of a tyrannical king learned to appreciate the might of even yeoman soldiers when committed to the defence of a righteous cause. Members of Davis's company were in many of the battles of the Revolution; and one of those upon whom Davis's blood fell went through the whole war, and said, that, wherever he went, he seemed to see that blood upon his clothes, urging him to do his duty.

As citizens of Acton, we enter into the spirit of this occasion most heartily. Most fitting is it that we should eulogize the courage of those men, who, one hundred years ago,

"Fired the shot heard round the world."

Fitting it is that a monument should mark the spot where these heroes fought and fell. And as the citizens of Acton were alive to a sense of their duty, and active in the performance of it on the 19th of April, 1775, and again on the 19th of April, 1861, so we trust that in love of country, and devotion to her defence, we ever may prove ourselves to be not unworthy descendants or townsmen of those whose memories we honor on this occasion, which is in itself memorable.

The President: I am now going to read to you a very few lines, but they tell a story to the American heart more touching than any thing to be drawn from ancient history; and the beautiful simplicity of the style should make it a classic. When, in her extreme old age, the widow of Captain Isaac Davis, who fell at the North Bridge, was seeking to obtain from Congress a pension for her husband's services on that day, her deposition was taken; and she told this story under oath. I will try to get through with reading it; but I never did yet without breaking down.

DEPOSITION OF CAPT. DAVIS'S WIDOW.

"I, Hannah Leighton of Acton, testify that I am eighty-nine years of age. Isaac Davis, who was killed in the Concord fight, in 1775, was my husband. He was then thirty years of age. We had four children, the youngest about fifteen months old. They were all unwell when he left me in the morning, some of them with the canker-rash. The alarm was given early in the morning. My husband lost no time in getting ready to go to Concord with his company. A considerable number of them came to the house, and made their cartridges there. The sun was from one to two hours high when they marched for Concord. My husband said but little that morning: he seemed serious and thoughtful, but never seemed to hesitate as to the course of his duty. As he led the company from the house, he turned round, and seemed to have something to communicate. He only said, "Take good care of the children," and was soon out of sight. In the afternoon, he was brought home a corpse. He was placed in my bedroom until the funeral. His countenance was pleasant, and seemed little altered. The bodies of Abner Hosmer and of James Hayward, one of the militia company who was killed in Lexington in the afternoon, were brought by their friends to the house, where the funeral of the three was attended.

HANNAH LEIGHTON."

Undoubtedly, fellow-citizens, every one of the thirty-one towns whose inhabitants participated in the events of the 19th of April, 1775, would have a story to tell, and would desire that the heroes of their own neighborhood should receive particular honor. We cannot, the time will not suffice to, render the tribute to them in detail and succession that we would gladly do. In their own towns, among their kindred and descendants, their memories and names are fresh. But to-day the names of Lexington and Concord must suffice for all. We take as our model, in this respect, the old Greek epigram : —

> "Athenian Æschylus, Euphorion's son,
> Buried at Gela's fields these lines declare:
> His deeds are registered at Marathon,
> Known to the deep-haired Mede, who met him there."

On the battle-ground from the North Bridge to Charlestown Neck, the men of the Massachusetts towns in arms did their duty and finished their work. Whoever died on that day, standing in arms for his country's defence, is a sharer in the glories of the fight and the victory.

We have been honored to-day by the presence of the Chief Executive Magistrate of the Commonwealth, of his Council, of the Legislature, of a large number of the high officers of the state. With our entire consent that a due share of the distinction of their official presence might be given to the celebration at Lexington, they have left us to join with our friends in that town in their solemn ceremonies. But I invite to respond, on behalf of the State of Massachusetts, on this occasion, our senior Senator, Gov. Boutwell, whom I am happy to see at our table.

ADDRESS OF HON. GEORGE S. BOUTWELL.

MR. PRESIDENT, LADIES, AND GENTLEMEN, — The events which we commemorate to-day I had occasion to consider a quarter of a century ago ; and one fact I venture to reproduce, because it is a great fact in our history and a great fact in the history of the republic. In June, 1776, when Maryland debated whether she would agree to the Declaration of Independence,

Acton, in town meeting assembled, first of all organized communities on this continent, declared for an American Republic, and said upon the record, "This is the only form of government we desire to see established."

I shall not review the events of the contest which began on the nineteenth day of April, 1775. That day is ranked justly with the great days of American history. Its claim to this distinction is admitted. The essential facts on which the claim is based belong to that day, and they relate to no other day. Therefore its honors cannot be divided, its right cannot be questioned, its pre-eminence cannot be denied. It stands alone. Like the day of the Declaration of Independence, it has no rivals. But this eminence of equality in fame with the Fourth of July is not due to the events of the day. The drama which opened at Lexington, and was continued to Concord, and there, with characters changed and conditions reversed, was re-enacted on the highway from Concord to Boston, could never have rendered the day illustrious, nor even have made it memorable for a century in the traditions and annals of a thoughtful people.

Three municipalities contend for the honor and glory of the day; and to those three municipalities the honor and glory of the day are first and specially due. Whether shared equally or unequally, enough of just fame belongs to each to stimulate the ambition of every generation to cherish, improve, and defend the institutions of the country, which their ancestors had so large a part in founding. But the ultimate justice of mankind counts nothing heroic or noble in action, that does not proceed from right principles and virtuous purposes. Therefore the actors in the events of the 19th of April are not to be judged now nor hereafter by what they did, but by the opinions they held, and by the character of the ends they sought. Of them it can be said that they had no love of military glory. They never sought distinction on the field of battle. But their principles and their purposes, they made known. The political life of Massachusetts was not a secret. It had been declared, it had been laid open indeed, in the convincing statements and unanswerable arguments of its House of Representatives addressed to the provincial governors, through a controversy of ten years. The principles and purposes of the colonists had been more than once set forth by the inhabitants of the town of Boston in their public meetings; and especially they had been declared by the people of the county of Middlesex, and never better than by the people of the county of Middlesex, by their representatives in convention assembled at Concord, in August, 1774.

First, as Englishmen they claimed the rights and liberties of Englishmen; and then, secondly, they claimed the rights and liberties of Englishmen, not only because they were Englishmen, but for the higher and better reason that they were men, and therefore could not be deprived justly of those rights and liberties by any power whatsoever.

The world had before seen many contests against oppression and tyranny, because oppression and tyranny were disagreeable; but it had never before seen a contest for liberty, because liberty was a common human right. It was on the breath of liberty that the shot fired at Concord was heard around the world; and its echoes will never cease to disturb the dreams of tyrants, until liberty and equality — the child of liberty — are the possession of all.

By this the 19th of April, 1775, was rendered illustrious; and for this the 19th of April, 1775, is memorable in the traditions and annals of a thoughtful people.

The President: Thank God, fellow-citizens, that the sun of the Hundredth Anniversary of the Nineteenth of April, 1775, through our broad land, has neither risen upon a master, nor will it set upon a slave!

I have to remind you that the people of New England were ready for the occurrences of the 19th of April, whenever they should happen, for a long time previous. The historical fact may not be known to many of you, that there was a false alarm, which came pretty near bringing on the conflict at a much pleasanter season of the year, when we should not have been so chilly in celebrating it. Governor Gage seized a part of the Province stores, which were deposited in the edge of Charlestown, up near Winter Hill, on the 1st of September, 1774; and the fact that he had seized the powder was circulated through the Colony, and through the adjoining Colonies. And what happened? Singularly enough, almost as if prophetic, the report accompanied this notice, that the soldiers had fired upon the people, and killed six of them. "The militia of Worcester County" (I read from the historian of America), "hearing of the removal of the powder belonging to the Province, rose *en masse*, and began the march to Boston. On Friday afternoon and Saturday morning, volunteers from Hampshire County advanced eastward as far as Shrewsbury. On the smallest computation, twenty thousand men were in motion. The rumor of the seizure reached Israel Putnam in Connecticut, with the addition that the British troops had fired on the people, and killed six men at the first shot. Sending forward the report to Norwich, New London, New Haven, New York, and so to Philadelphia, he summoned the neighboring militia to take up arms. Thousands started at his call; but these, like the volunteers of Massachusetts, were stopped by expresses from the patriots of Boston, who sent word that at present nothing was to be attempted."

On this national occasion we are honored by the presence of all the Governors of New England, and of one or more of the Governors of the other thirteen original states. The Governor of South Carolina has been with us to-day; and I am sorry he is not present now to address you. He has gone to Lexington. But I will invite the honored Governor of the State of Connecticut, whose citizens were ready, under General Putnam, to respond with such alacrity a hundred years ago, to let us know that that state shares in the glory of the opening of the Revolution. Allow me to present to the audience Governor Ingersoll of Connecticut.

ADDRESS OF GOVERNOR INGERSOLL.

FELLOW-CITIZENS, — I am at a loss fittingly to acknowledge the honor which your distinguished President has done my state. It is some comfort, however, to know, that, when a Massachusetts man speaks in praise of Connecticut, he receives some portion of his reward as he goes along; for his praise of Connecticut reflects upon Massachusetts, whose child she was. The three vines which I see yonder, and which, for nearly two centuries and a half, have typified our fruitful existence, are only offshoots of that parent vine which was planted when the heathen were cast out of Massachusetts Bay. You know, Mr. President, how those offshoots came to shoot off. It was a long time after the promised land in the valley of the Connecticut was discovered before the restless colonists could make up their minds to emigrate. The mother colony was very strongly averse to such a secession; and, for many months of prayerful worry, the question hung in the scales, until, finally, an event occurred which caused the scale to kick the beam. The General Court of Massachusetts resolved that they should not go; and being the children of Massachusetts, why, nothing else was needed to determine them to go; and they went. And then sagacious Massachusetts, when she found that they were determined to go, resolved, in her General Court, that they might go, provided only that they would remain under the jurisdiction of her General Court. The only reply, Mr. President, that was ever made to that was the vote, which, from that day to this, has remained as the cornerstone of the government of Connecticut. "We have established a Commonwealth, the supreme power of which, under Almighty God, is in the freemen of our General Court." It was the first declaration of independence on this continent. It was the beginning of constitutional government in modern times. And, Mr. President, that has a significance for this occasion. For, when old mother Massachusetts found her troubles gathering thick and fast about her one hundred years ago, she found at her right hand this rebel offspring, equipped as no other British colony was equipped, — with a government all its own, automatic; with every official, from Brother Jonathan down, the choice of her own freemen; with her treasury in her own keeping, her militia subject to her own order, and, back of all, a body of freemen instinct with this inherited spirit of independence. In our generation we have seen patriotic uprisings; but we have seen nothing equal to what we hear as having occurred at that time in Connecticut, and to which allusion has just been made so touchingly by your President. When the tidings came, albeit by a false alarm, that the British general had seized upon Boston Town with his military arm, fully one half of the arms-bearing population of Connecticut were on the roads leading to Massachusetts Bay. And when the tidings finally came in truth, that blood had been spilled in the streets of your village, why, every function of the government of Connecticut was set in motion. Her Governor set the militia at work. Within eighteen hours from the time that Putnam, then a major-general of her militia, heard at Pomfret, one hundred miles away, the tidings, he was in the streets of Concord. More than that: from the treasury of Connecticut was then organized that expedition which struck the first aggressive blow against the power of Great Britain, and brought down Ticonderoga and Crown Point, "in the name of the Great Jehovah and the Continental Congress."

This day, Mr. President and gentlemen, is therefore historic in the annals of Connecticut as it is in the annals of Massachusetts. It commenced with us a period from which, for many anxious years, war was the business of Connecticut for the accomplishment of that great seminal principle of New England political life, — the right of self-government. That is the gift which America has given to the nineteenth century. It rules the civilized world to-day. Wherever you may look, whatever may be the form of government, public opinion, whether expressed in the ballot, or by any of the manifold agencies of modern civilization, rules to day every government in Christendom.

Mr. President, it is pardonable, and perhaps expected, that, on an occasion of this sort, I should indulge in a little vain glory. I fear that I may have abused my privilege. But I thank you for your kind attention.

Music.

The President: Fellow-citizens, what has been said by our friend, the Governor of Connecticut, reminds me that a part of New England was not a state, or even a colony, or a province in 1775, — and what it was, except the residence of a set of pretty sturdy patriots, who meant to manage the place where they lived in their own way, I do not know that I can describe, — but it is now the State of Vermont. It was then a place that was carried on "in the name of the Great Jehovah and the Continental Congress." The Governor of that State has honored us with his presence; and, as in the case of the Governor of Connecticut, he has brought with him a splendid military company, as an escort, to decorate our festivities. I introduce Governor Peck of Vermont.

ADDRESS OF GOVERNOR PECK.

Mr. President, Ladies, and Gentlemen, — I will not undertake to add any thing to the masterly expositions which have been given to-day of the principles involved in the event which we commemorate. I fear, if I should attempt to do so, it would be but throwing dust in the face of the sun. But in the maintenance of those principles I have simply to say that Vermont, I trust, in every emergency, will be true to the motto which she has engraven upon her seal, "Freedom and Unity." And a guaranty for that is the tried patriotism of her people, and the history of her soldiery from Ticonderoga to Appomattox.

Allow me, Mr. President, simply to express the thanks in my own behalf, and in behalf of the people who have accompanied me on this memorial occasion, for the courteous reception which we have received at the hands of the citizens of Concord and its vicinity. And allow me to say that we shall ever cherish, and remember with pleasure, the visit from my beloved Green Mountain State, which was the cradle of my infancy, to the good old Commonwealth of Massachusetts, the State of my birth.

The President: The men of New Hampshire were on their way to Concord and Lexington before night on the 19th of April, 1775. New Hampshire has honored us to-day with her official presence, and the presence of her citizen-soldiers. I will call on Governor Weston of New Hampshire.

Governor Weston not appearing, the President continued, —

I am afraid the propensity that was so highly developed in the people of this region on the 19th of April, 1775, to follow down on the track of the British to Boston, has taken away a good many of our friends from whom we should be glad to hear.

The Governor of a state from which Massachusetts was set off about fifty years ago has come up to take the part of that state in the old ancestral glories, and brought us that beautiful company, the Portland Mechanic Blues, as his guard on this occasion. I hope that Governor Dingley will allow the audience to hear a few words from him.

ADDRESS OF GOVERNOR DINGLEY.

Mr. President, — At this late hour, it is hardly fitting that I should occupy more time than simply to thank you for the courtesy which has permitted my presence as the representative of the State of Maine upon this occasion.

But, sir, you have been pleased to refer to the state which I have the honor to represent, as having, a half-century since, separated from the parent Commonwealth of Massachusetts. My friend, the Governor of Connecticut, was pleased to say, a few moments since, that Connecticut was the child of Massachusetts returning to the old homestead. Sir, I have to remind you on this occasion, that while Maine is proud to proclaim herself the child of Massachusetts, yet, sir, she did not leave the old homestead until the parent Commonwealth was free from her troubles, and could allow the children to leave home in safety.

It is, indeed, a pleasant thought to me (and I but express the feelings of the people of the State of Maine, whom I represent on this occasion), that her sons stood by you in the days that tried men's souls; that the glories of Massachusetts were her glories, and your battle-fields were her battle-fields. It is indeed grateful to me, and a memory which the people of the State of Maine cherish, that old Massachusetts is their mother; that Concord is hers, that Lexington is hers, that Bunker Hill is hers.

My friends, accept my thanks for the courtesy extended, and permit me to hope that the feelings which have here been indulged, the words which have here been expressed, and the patriotic thoughts which have here been uttered, may go from one end of this Union to the other, animating the heart of every citizen, and binding the people of this nation more closely together in love and friendship.

The President: There is one more New England State, fellow-citizens, the little State of Rhode Island. I do not know that our friends from that state will like to have that adjective precede the name: so I will say the *great* State of Rhode Island. I regret that the Executive of that state has been obliged to leave us too early to respond to the honorable notice which we wished to take of their Commonwealth on this occasion. I had hoped, in his absence, that I might be able to call upon a man, who, I think, is now seeking to achieve some celebrity as *Major* Burnside of the Providence Light Infantry. He has been here in command of that body to-day; probably a command, which, for this purpose, is as high as anybody's; but I think I have heard the name before on some larger fields, if not of more historic celebrity. But with the natural desire to "kill two birds with one stone," and with the feeling that Rhode Island — a state which undertook to commence the Revolution about three years before it began, and pretty nearly did it, sending out, one day in 1772, an expedition of whale-boats to seize the "Gaspee" — should be heard from on this occasion, it was borne in upon me that our friend whose magnificent oration has stirred our souls, and touched our hearts, to-day, — although I introduced him as a man whose youth was spent in Concord, and who is now an eminent citizen of New York, — is a native of Rhode Island. I rather think he has some quality which would enable him adequately to represent any state in the Union. I introduce the orator of the day, Mr. Curtis.

ADDRESS OF GEORGE WILLIAM CURTIS.

MR. PRESIDENT, AND FELLOW-CITIZENS OF CONCORD, OF MIDDLESEX COUNTY, OF MASSACHUSETTS, OF THE UNION, — I see, what you may not, the deep malevolence of the President of the Day. For as he knows that in the unequal contest of my voice with a hundred bands of music and a cracking platform, that voice got irretrievably the worst of it, in revenge for holding so many of my fellow-citizens for more than an hour in the cold, the President of the Day, with malicious intent, is resolved to make an end of that voice altogether. But, sir, when the name of Rhode Island is mentioned, every son of Rhode Island falls into line. Little in size, but great in soul! Like the minute-men of one hundred years ago, who marched to the North Bridge under three leaders, so Rhode Island always marches under her three historical men, — Roger Williams, Dr. Channing, and Gen. Greene, the friend of Washington. Little in size, but great in soul! for the founder of Rhode Island was the first man among the founders of States who ever asserted absolute religious liberty as the truest foundation of human society.

Fellow-citizens, as I stand here in Middlesex County on a day devoted to Revolutionary remembrances, it is my pleasure to remember that when the first regiment from Massachusetts marched to the late war, when it was passing through the city of New York, a friend of mine joined a soldier on the march, and said to him, "Well, my friend, what part of the old Commonwealth do you come from?" And that soldier, whose ear for music, I take it, was not very good, anxious to answer the question while he still kept time to the drum-beat, answered my friend as he marched on, "From Bunker Hill, from Bunker Hill, from Bunker Hill." And so, fellow-citizens, I think we may take this lesson from this day, and the spot on which we stand, — that every American citizen, whatever the summons may be, when it is a summons to march for liberty, may reply, when asked from what part of this Union he takes his departure, not from Maine, from Florida, from Massachusetts, from Rhode Island, from Virginia, from Illinois, from Nevada, from Oregon: let him say only, "From Concord Bridge, from Concord Bridge, from Concord Bridge," and then the whole world will know that he, too, is marching to victory.

The President: I hope it will be always as true as it was one hundred years ago, if a man should be asked, when he is marching to fight or die in the service of his country, from what part of Massachusetts he came, that he might answer, "From the whole of it;" and it would not be a very hard thing to say of Rhode Island.

We have here, to which I must call attention, a good many Revolutionary relics. You have had already shown to you what is left of the sword — broken off, a foot of it, and the point sharpened — that Isaac Davis carried at the North Bridge. There is before me a sword taken by Nathaniel Bemis of Watertown from a British officer whom he himself shot; and the gun is here with which he shot him. The sword bears the legend, and the gun has on the breech, "David Bemis, 1775." But, gentlemen, I hold in my hand one sacred relic, whose historic glory is unsurpassed. Little local jealousies may exist among neighboring towns as to the particular share that this or that spot had in this great American day. The title of Concord North Bridge rests upon one unquestioned fact: that there first, by a duly commissioned officer in command of soldiers, an order to the soldiers of the people to fire upon the soldiers of the King was given, and was obeyed. Major John Buttrick of Concord, whose gun I hold in my hand, gave the order to fire, and fired this gun, his own gun that he held in his hand, in execution of his own order; and it was the first gun fired in obedience to military authority in the war of the Revolution. Fifty years ago, when Lafayette visited the United States, this gun was shown to him, and this story told him. He grasped and held it up over his head, and said it was "*the* alarum gun of liberty throughout the world."

I have already said to you that I considered the independence of America as assured by what took place between the North Bridge and Charlestown Neck one hundred years ago. It made conciliation impossible, and independence certain. Lord Chatham had already prophesied in the British parliament, in January, 1775, that the first drop of blood shed in civil and unnatural war might be a wound that never could be cured. He put into that speech a recommendation to the ministry, which, read in the light of this day, sounds curiously enough, although not in the meaning which he gave to it. He introduced into the British parliament a resolution calling on the King to withdraw his troops from Boston. It did not pass: it received but a few votes in the House of Lords. In the course of that speech, he said that he advised the ministry "to make the first advances to Concord." And Gen. Gage made them. You know how they turned out.

Now, my friends, although this, as we all know, is the great centennial, some allusion was made by the orator, in an oratorical spirit, undoubtedly, to the Fourth of July. He knows that comes this year and next, and we think very well of the Fourth of July. It is a natural deduction from the 19th of April; and whoever gets the spirit of the 19th of April may be trusted anywhere on the Fourth of July. My friend General Hawley, late Governor Hawley of Connecticut, entitled to memory as General Hawley of the late war, Chairman of the National Centennial Commission, is here; and I am sure, if anybody can say any thing in favor of the Fourth of July, he can say it, and I should like to hear from him on that subject.

ADDRESS OF GENERAL HAWLEY.

Mr. Chairman and Fellow-Citizens, — I am very much obliged to Mr. Boutwell and the Chairman for the few kind words they have said for the Fourth of July. I began to fear it hadn't any friends, even in old Massachusetts. The temptation to every speaker is, of course, to dwell somewhat upon the day, and the events that belong to it. I must pass that by for the duty more especially devolving upon myself.

I was just looking at a newspaper account of the circumstances that followed, in my own State, this 19th of April, as the courier, Isaac Bissell, galloped down through the State of Connecticut, getting a fresh horse in every town, and receiving upon his paper the receipt of some of the leading citizens. The alarm spread through the State; and forty-seven towns started out ninety-three companies, containing thirty-six hundred men, for Boston. In many cases, citizens started out alone. I know the story of old James McLane, young James McLane then, of Glastenbury. He was one of the minute-men our orators have so grandly described. I suppose he was not a great scholar or learned man. Perhaps he ought to have stopped to think about this: he ought to have reflected, that, in some mysterious way, culture would redeem this world without fighting, and remained at home, and smoked his pipe. But James was a plain man. His gun was out of order: his new shoes were not ready. James went over to his shoemaker, and told him they must be done before night. He walked five miles to a gunsmith's, and had his musket put in order; and the next morning, with his new shoes and repaired musket, and a proper allowance of powder and ball, James started for Boston, and came home at the end of the war as Captain James McLane. He was one of the minute-men, one of the thirty-six hundred that Connecticut started as soon as she got the word. And, wherever Massachusetts was found in the struggle, Connecticut was by her side.

But I must not dwell upon the reminiscences that come into my mind in connection with these events. I am very glad of the opportunity to say a word to you concerning the great International Exposition and National Celebration next year. It was inevitable that there should be such a celebration. You could not have kept Concord and Lexington from celebrating this day. But, while we all claim a certain share in it, the nation has adopted the Fourth of July as the national holiday, the great day in which all these glories are garnered into one, the prophesied day of John Adams, of bonfires and illuminations and bell-ringing.

You could not have carried this people by it without some sort of national celebration. It became quite appropriate and natural that there should be on that day, to apply, perhaps, a phrase below the dignity of the affair, something like taking an account of stock of our possessions and our great progress, — a comparison of the America of 1876 with the America of 1776. You know we should have got not only this interesting collection of relics, but thousands of others like them, representing the progress of the whole art of war up to that time, — the great guns and the small guns, and the ships and implements of war; and quite naturally we should have placed by their side the implements which would be used in a war to-day, — the improved guns, the modern appliances, the models of our ships; and we should have had a great exhibition. Here is a part of it now. When you begin to talk of a national celebration, you will fill a building with things of this kind.

But there is a new battle to be fought, a new time coming. The work of the next century is not to be the work of the last. The world is to be better one hundred years hence than it is now. The time was one hundred years ago when you must pour out blood to save the right. We will learn in the next one hundred years to save the blood and the right also, that the world may live in peace. The arts of peace are to be glorified. Massachusetts does not look backward forever, but only to take inspiration for the future. We shall gather in this great exhibition all that shows our prowess in a hundred battle-fields. The soldier is not king always. I take off my hat when I go into the great machine-shops, in the presence of my master, the mechanic of the nineteenth century. Now we want in this exhibition samples of the skill of the workmen in the textile fabrics, in iron and steel, the work of the painter and sculptor, specimens of our soils and minerals: we want collected there everything that will show the wonderful resources of this continent, and to ask all our people to come together during those six months, and shake hands, and thank God for what he has done for us, and take courage for the future.

I might dwell upon the material benefits of this exposition; but, as I have thought of it, its moral benefits rise still greater to my sight. You cannot meet here without some necessity for shaking hands over some of the old dissensions. I find Lexington a little jealous of Concord, and Concord of Lexington, and Acton of both; and you have these little controversies and disputes. When the great War of Independence was over, your towns were full of Tories; and you had to be reconciled to them. We in this country have been through a struggle, of which we cannot speak without great pride, to be sure, and gratitude to Almighty God; but so terrible was it, that no man approached the thought of it but with the most serious reflections. We want, in this great celebration and exhibition of 1876, all our Southern friends there, that we may shake hands with the men of the South. Reconciliations are not always made by orations and by platforms, by letters and addresses. When you have quarrelled with your brother, it is often just as well to say nothing, but let the eye and the hand settle it, and let the past be buried. Our friends of the South will not contribute greatly to the material display of that exhibition; but we of the North must do it largely, mostly. But let from Massachusetts, from New England, from all the North, go out such a voice of welcome and entreaty to them to come, that they must be there.

The influence of the exhibition is not confined to this land alone. Having a national exhibition, and having been invited to all the national ones on the Eastern Continent, we could not hold one without inviting foreigners; and they are coming from the great civilized nations, and from many we have treated as half-civilized and barbarous. They are all coming; some with a display that will astonish you in your pride as American mechanics and artists. You may lose something of your vanity; but you can be instructed and benefited. They will be there as our fellow-men, as our friends. Our British friends will be there with a great display. In the first place, they cannot afford to stay away from this, their great market. In the second place, their good-will is with us to-day. There is not a statesman in that land who does not think it is just as well that we left them at the time we did, and is not proud of us, as an English-speaking nation, with rights and liberties born of English soil. They are our friends and neighbors.

The theme enlarges as you dwell upon it. Massachusetts has had the glory of leading off in the great series of centennial celebrations. I beg of Massachusetts men to take into consideration the great national celebration of 1876. We have in process of construction over fifty acres of buildings on the finest site ever selected for such a purpose. Our contracts are made for the earliest construction with the heaviest penalties. There never was so fine an arrangement made for bringing goods and people together as under those roofs. The exhibition, I tell you seriously, will be the finest the world has ever seen. It may be one hundred per cent better than we think it will be, if you say it is to be, and the world will come and see. Your national honor is committed to it; and let America see that the exhibition is not one that she can in any respect be ashamed of.

The President: On the 22d of August, 1775, the overseers of Harvard College met, and, having read the report of a committee previously appointed, unanimously voted, "That it is of great importance that the education of the youth in this Colony in piety and good literature should be carried on with as little interruption as may be; that the education of the scholars of Harvard College cannot be carried on at Cambridge while the war in which we have been forced to engage for the defence of our liberties shall continue; and, therefore, that it is necessary that some other place should be speedily appointed for that purpose." The committee, reported as their opinion, that Concord was a town suitable for the purpose; and one of the results of the 19th of April was the removal of Harvard College from Cambridge to Concord, where it staid about a year The chill of the weather, I am afraid, has deprived me of the opportunity of calling upon President Eliot of Harvard College to reply to the following sentiment: —

Harvard College: Its founding was said to have hastened the American Revolution fifty years.

Now, fellow-citizens, there are but two things more to which I wish to ask your attention before parting. I cannot go over these relics lying on the table before me, in detail. We have a pair of scissors with which all the cartridges were cut that were used here on the 19th of April, 1775; and the son of the young lady who used them at that time has sent them on. He mended them himself sixty-three years ago, and had them from his mother with their curious story. Here is, also, an old silver tankard of the date of 1700, that was buried in a barrel of soft soap when the British came to Concord in 1775, by way of preservation. Here are, also, powder-horns, swords, and guns, which were borne on that day. In the procession to-day, carried by the town of Bedford, has been a flag which was carried on the 19th of April, 1775.

As a close to the particular memories of the occasion, I wish to give you as a sentiment: —

Lexington and Concord, and the memory of Col. James Barrett, Major John Buttrick, and Lieut. Col. John Robinson.

> "In pride, in all the pride of woe,
> We tell of them, the brave laid low,
> Who for their birthplace bled:
> In pride, the pride of triumph then,
> We tell of them, the matchless men
> From whom the invaders fled."

We have received from men eminent in public station, and honored throughout the country, many letters in reply to invitations to be present, which it would have given me pleasure to read to the assembled company. But the chill in the air has been too much for us; and I will not detain you by reading more than one. That one is of such a representative character in connection with the memories of this occasion, that I desire to lay it before you now. It begins with an excuse by the writer, for having failed to receive his invitation seasonably enough to make arrangements to attend.

"WASHINGTON, April 16, 1875.

. . . .

Please consider me as sincerely grateful for the honor implied in the invitation extended me, and accept my best wishes for the success of the proposed celebration. The opening of the Revolutionary War was the opening of this continent to a higher and purer liberty than the world had known before, — a liberty in presence of which no privileged classes of wealth or religion, race or color, can long endure.

Fully appreciating the kindness and significance of the invitation extended me, I am,

With great respect, yours truly,

FREDERICK DOUGLASS."

If there is any one of our friends who desires to add a word, or has any particular suggestion or memory, I invite him now to address you: otherwise he will have to await his next opportunity at the next centennial, at which I am very sure I shall not preside.

A Citizen: May I be allowed to repeat a sentiment which was given fifty years ago to-day by a citizen of this town? It was this:—

"*The Tree of Liberty:* May it take deep root, and grow until its branches shall cover the whole earth."

The exercises then closed, and the company dispersed.

From the many letters received from distinguished men, accepting the invitation to attend the celebration, or regretting their inability to be present, the following are selected for publication: —

WASHINGTON, D.C., April 3, 1875.

GENTLEMEN, — It is with much regret, that, in behalf of my brethren and myself, I write to say, that it will be out of our power to accept the invitation of the inhabitants of the town of Concord to unite with them in celebrating the centennial anniversary of the opening of the Revolutionary War.

I beg you to be assured, that nothing less than the demands of the very important business, which requires the attention of the court before its adjournment on the third of next month, could have induced us to forego the pleasure of participating in the commemoration of that great historical event on the spot where it came to pass.

Very gratefully yours,
M. R. WAITE.

MESSRS. E. R. HOAR, R. W. EMERSON, G. HEYWOOD, *Committee.*

HEADQUARTERS ARMY OF THE UNITED STATES,
ST. LOUIS, MO., Dec. 7, 1874.

GENTLEMEN, — I have the honor to acknowledge the receipt of your beautiful card of invitation to be present as the guest of the town of Concord, Mass., on the 19th of April, 1875, to assist in celebrating the centennial anniversary of the opening event of the Revolutionary War.

Although a slip which accompanies the card does not contemplate an answer earlier than April 1, 1875, I cannot risk the delay, lest it then be overlooked, and prefer now to thank you truly for including my name among the honored guests. I can hardly promise myself the pleasure to share in the festivities of the occasion; but I assure you, that, if I happen to be east of the Alleghany Mountains next spring, I will endeavor to time my visit so as to see the place where the people first had the hardihood to defend with arms their property against a detachment of the British army.[1]

With great respect, most truly your friend,
W. T. SHERMAN, *General.*

MESSRS. E. R. HOAR, R. W. EMERSON, GEO. HEYWOOD, *Committee.*

AMESBURY, MASS., 12th 4th mo., 1875.

GENTLEMEN, — Your invitation to the celebration of the centennial anniversary of the opening of the Revolutionary War, in Concord, has been received.

It will not be in my power to accept your invitation. Lifelong habit and the state of my health, alike deter me from joining the great multitude which the occasion will call together. As a son of Massachusetts, and as a friend of human freedom, I am not insensible to the associations of the place and the time. I recognize and rejoice in the results of the great struggle commenced in two small villages of my native state one hundred years ago.

---

[1] Pursuant to the promise contained in this letter Gen. Sherman visited Concord on June 18, 1875, and was received by the Committee of Arrangements, and escorted to the battle-ground by a large body of citizens.

But I am sure you will unite with me in the hope, that, long before the next centennial of the event which has made your town famous the world over, all disputes of governments and peoples will be referred to peaceful arbitrament, and nation shall not lift up sword against nation, nor the people learn war any more. I am very truly your friend,

JOHN G. WHITTIER.

To E. R. HOAR, R. W. EMERSON, G. HEYWOOD, *Committee.*

HEADQUARTERS MILITARY DIVISION OF THE ATLANTIC,
NEW YORK, 13th April, 1875.

GENTLEMEN, — I have the honor to acknowledge the receipt of your polite invitation to myself and staff to be the guests of the inhabitants of Concord on the 19th inst., and to join with them in celebrating the centennial anniversary of the opening of the Revolutionary War.

The occasion is one of deep interest to every American. Nothing was permitted by the minute-men of Concord to interfere with their performance of great deeds. To take part in commemorating the services of these pioneers of our liberties is an honor and a pleasure that I only forego with sincere regret.

But a recent domestic affliction will not permit my acceptance of your kind invitation; nor will it be practicable for the members of my staff to be present.

With the highest appreciation of the compliment paid to myself and staff, I have the honor to be, gentlemen,

Your very obedient servant,

WINFIELD S. HANCOCK, *Major-General, U. S. A.*

To MESSRS. E. R. HOAR, R. W. EMERSON, GEO. HEYWOOD,
Committee of Invitations, &c., Concord, Mass.

COMMONWEALTH OF VIRGINIA, GOVERNOR'S OFFICE,
RICHMOND, April 15, 1875.

SIR, — Official engagements will prevent me from uniting with you on the 19th inst., in celebrating the one hundredth anniversary of the opening of the Revolutionary War.

As the hundredth anniversary of the birth of the republic approaches, it is my devout hope — and it is, undoubtedly, the ardent aspiration of the Southern people — that the patriotism of our great ancestors shall be re-awakened, that sectional animosities shall disappear forever, that the last of the Federal statutes which prejudice or impair the full co-equality of the states shall be swept from existence, and that the original purity and simplicity of the government shall return with real peace, prosperity, and fraternity to every section. I have the honor to be,

Very respectfully yours,

JAMES L. KEMPER.

SAMUEL HOAR, Esq., *Sec. Com. of Arrangements, Concord, Mass.*

WASHINGTON, D.C., March 22, 1875.

GENTLEMEN, — I gratefully acknowledge your invitation to be present as the guest of the inhabitants of Concord on the 19th of April next, on the occasion of celebrating the centennial anniversary of the opening of the Revolutionary War. I am sincerely sorry that engagements indispensable will prevent me from having the pleasure of being present on that great interesting occasion.

I think that no American whose heart beats time to that noblest music of resistance to tyranny, and of liberty under law, can fail to feel proud emotions as he looks back over one hundred years to that great day, and measures the ever renewed and beneficent harvest of progress for our country and our race, that has ripened from the blood of martyrs shed on that day. Civil liberty, tolerance of religious opinion, the separation of Church and State, order, equal rights under the reign of republican law, have, as it seems to me, all been touched, and warmed into stronger life, by the fires kindled on that single field. Well, then, may the inhabitants of your ancient town celebrate with pride and circumstance the century of results flowing from the conflict of the first battle-field of the republic. But not they alone: the nation itself, from the Atlantic to the shores of the tranquil ocean, should take up your rejoicings, and hold high festival everywhere, as a memorial of the men who laid the firm foundations of our great republic.

From my heart I say, All hail!   Very sincerely yours,

GEO. F. EDMUNDS.

THE HONS. E. R. HOAR, R. W. EMERSON, GEORGE HEYWOOD,
Committee of Invitation &c., Concord, Mass.

HARTFORD, CONN., March 31, 1875.

GENTLEMEN, — Your favor, covering an invitation to attend the centennial anniversary of the opening of the Revolutionary War, is at hand.

I beg you to accept my thanks, and regret that my engagements absolutely forbid my acceptance.

I have no doubt but a meeting such as Concord will have, upon an occasion so interesting, may be productive of good all over the Union, tending to bring back the era of good feeling and brotherly confidence and affection, which characterized our ancestors when Massachusetts and Virginia, South Carolina and Connecticut, stood shoulder to shoulder in defence of the principles of civil liberty.

May your celebration inaugurate anew the old affection!

Very sincerely, &c.,

WM. W. EATON.

MESSRS. E. R. HOAR, and Others.

INDIANAPOLIS, IND., April 16, 1875.

GENTLEMEN OF THE COMMITTEE OF INVITATION, — Your invitation to attend the celebration of the hundredth anniversary of the battle of Concord came to me at a time when I hoped to be able to attend; but I find that I cannot do so. It would be most gratifying to meet with the descendants of the patriots who first openly, in arms, resisted oppression, upon the very spot illustrated by their heroism, to commemorate their deeds by joining in the inauguration of a monument.

Looking backward to the few hardy and daring men who set the example to the people of the colonies, of resistance by force to oppression, we can, better than their contemporaries, appreciate the importance of their efforts. Some one must needs begin the struggle which was to end in revolution and desolating war; some one must strike the first blow; some one must sound the note that was to waken the American people to arms; and it was set apart by Providence that the people of Concord should do these illustrious deeds.

They were well done. The great procession of events that is still moving on dates back to that day and those men, as the beginning of our separate existence as a nation. Hoping, that, for ages and ages, a free and united people may yet meet to celebrate the deeds of the men of Concord,

I remain yours truly,

JOHN COBURN.

WOONSOCKET, R.I., April 9, 1875.

GENTLEMEN, — Please accept my thanks for the cordial invitation to join the inhabitants of Concord in celebrating the centennial anniversary of the opening of the Revolutionary War on the 19th inst., — an event which has inspired so many hearts to heroic efforts for liberty the world over.

I hope to make my arrangements so as to be present, and join the citizens of Concord on the hallowed occasion.

With high esteem, gratefully yours,

L. W. BALLOU.

To MESSRS. E. R. HOAR, R. W. EMERSON, GEO. HEYWOOD, *Committee.*

GLOUCESTER, MASS., April 10, 1875.

DEAR SIRS, — I have received, through you, an invitation from the inhabitants of the town of Concord to join with them on the nineteenth day of April, 1875, in celebrating the centennial anniversary of the opening of the Revolutionary War, and assure you I highly appreciate your kindness, and shall be with you on that occasion, if within my power to do so. The importance of the event you are to celebrate cannot be too highly estimated, nor the actors in it hold too high a place in our affections. The principles they fought to establish and vindicate were then, are now, and will remain, the true basis of all free governments, — equality of all men before the laws, the greatest personal liberty compatible with individual security, and local self-government. This is the foundation upon which they built the state. May we be as ready to maintain, at every hazard, the government upon that foundation, as they were to establish it. I am, with great respect for your inhabitants and their committee,

Truly their obedient servant,
CHARLES P. THOMPSON.

HONS. E. R. HOAR, R. W. EMERSON, GEO. HEYWOOD,
Committee, Concord, Mass.

CAMBRIDGE, MASS., April 9, 1875.

MY DEAR SIR, — I confess to great remissness of duty, as well as a lack of due courtesy, in delaying to answer the kind invitation of the committee to be present at the celebration in Concord on the approaching 19th of April.

I have been waiting to see if I could not make it consistent with duties and engagements elsewhere to accept the honor so kindly tendered me. But I cannot see my way clear to do so; and, to relieve the suspense, I am obliged reluctantly to decline, which, in view of the splendid promise of a celebration of unparalleled interest upon a spot of such historic fame, I cannot do, without repeating with how much regret I do it.

Very truly and respectfully, your obedient servant,
EMORY WASHBURN.

SAMUEL HOAR, ESQ., *Secretary, &c.*

WASHINGTON, D.C., April 9, 1875.

MY DEAR SIRS, — I regret I cannot be present at the centennial anniversary of the battle of Lexington and Concord. The occasion has every element of a national festival.

The encounter was not accidental, but the result of the principles and character of the people, transmitted from generation to generation. It was as much the flowering-out of a succession of ages as the Iliad of Homer, or the Cologne Cathedral. It might have happened in other villages in New England; but it could have happened only in a New-England country town.

It is said, that, when the Romans invaded Germany, an aged matron met them with the command, "Go back!" The word of command given on the hillock in Concord marks the moment when the measures of persecution and tyranny, devised under the Tudors and the Stuarts, began to recede; and the cause, which had been lost in the mother-country by Hampden and Cromwell, entered upon that career of success which was to help the mother-country itself to better institutions, and teach the true art of colonization to the world.

Yours most truly,
GEORGE BANCROFT.

HON. E. ROCKWOOD HOAR, and Other Members of the Committee of Invitations.

BOSTON, April 12, 1875.

GENTLEMEN, — For the cordial invitation to me, in behalf of the citizens of Concord, "to be present as their guest on the 19th of this month, and to join with them in celebrating the centennial anniversary of the opening of the Revolutionary War," I return my sincere thanks to them and to yourselves. Circumstances, however, will prevent my attendance.

The event to be commemorated, though only a local skirmish, bore such a relation to the seven-years' struggle for American independence as will forever invest it with historical interest and importance. Probably it was not given to any of those who participated in it to foresee what would be the consequences, beyond the peril of the hour, and the liability to seal with their blood their resistance to tyrannical dominion; but, with them, sufficient unto the day was failure or success, obscurity or renown. They were not battling for fame, but for freedom; and whether their patriotic uprising should afterward be deemed to possess only a local significance, or whether it should prove (as it did) what the early dawn is to the coming day, they knew not and cared not. One purpose, at least, animated their breasts: it was to be enrolled among

> "Men who their duties know,
> But know their rights, and, knowing, dare maintain,
> Prevent the long-aimed blow,
> And crush the tyrant while they rend the chain."

There are, indeed, various methods of assailing oppression, and maintaining the cause of liberty. As an advocate of peace, in a very radical sense, it would not be consistent for me to glory in the shedding of human blood, however desirable the end in view; yet in every conflict (however sanguinary) between the oppressors and the oppressed, — force against force, — all my sympathies, hopes, and best wishes have been, and will continue to be, with the down-trodden side. Men cannot exceed their highest convictions of duty; and if, in reducing them to practice, — though there may be a higher plane of action not yet attained, and nobler instrumentalities to be used, — there is shown a readiness to confront death itself in the service of freedom, they will be sure to have their self-sacrificing spirit crowned with respect and honor by mankind.

It is an easy matter to celebrate the deeds of such, and to be proud of them as ancestors. To make the occasion worthy of us, there should be drawn from it an admonitory lesson to chasten our exultation, — lessons of justice not yet enforced, of equal rights still denied, of national unity not yet attained. The Declaration of Independence still remains to be carried out in its fundamental principles and "self-evident truths." True, the atrocious system of chattel slavery has been abolished, and its victims nominally admitted to citizenship; but they still need to have their rights protected, and to be put in possession of all those privileges and immunities which are accorded even to aliens and foreigners on our soil. Moreover, in persistently denying to one half of our population (solely on the ground of sex) all political power, all representation in legislative and municipal assemblies, all voice in the enactment and administration of the laws, and classifying them in an opprobrious manner, we are trampling under foot our own heaven-attested declaration, that "governments derive their just powers from the consent of the governed," and, in imitation of the mother-country under George the Third, imposing taxation, but denying the right of representation. This great injustice must be removed.

Very respectfully yours,

WM. LLOYD GARRISON.

MESSRS. E. R. HOAR, R. W. EMERSON, GEO. HEYWOOD,
Committee of Invitation.

NEW YORK, April 3, 1875.

GENTLEMEN, — I regret extremely that inexorable engagements will prevent me from accepting the invitation of the inhabitants of the town of Concord " to join with them in celebrating the centennial anniversary of the opening of the Revolutionary War."

My personal associations from early childhood, with this ancient town, and my familiar acquaintance ever since, with some of its distinguished inhabitants, would increase the interest of the approaching celebration to me, as they do my regret at not being able to take part in it.

With profound thanks to the town for the honor it has done me by the invitation, I am, gentlemen, your obedient servant,

WM. M. EVARTS.

TO THE COMMITTEE.

FARMINGTON AVENUE, HARTFORD, March 6.

GENTLEMEN, — I offer my thanks to the citizens of Concord for their courteous invitation, and shall be glad indeed to be present on the 19th of April, and assist in laying the last stone of the basement story of American history. Very truly yours,

SAML. L. CLEMENS.

TO HON. E. R. HOAR, R. W. EMERSON, ESQ., GEO. HEYWOOD, ESQ.,
Committee, &c.

PHILADELPHIA, April 3, 1875.

GENTLEMEN, — Your note conveying the invitation of the inhabitants of the town of Concord, Massachusetts, to be present with them as their guest on the 19th of April next, and to join with them in celebrating the centennial anniversary of the memorable and momentous event of which their town was the scene on the 19th of April, 1775, has been received, and, appreciating the high compliment thus rendered, I thank you, and those whom you represent, and gratefully accept the invitation.

Regarding the day to be commemorated as a decisive epoch in the history of liberty in the American world, its celebration can hardly fail to be productive of the best results in recalling to us of the present generation the sound principles of the great men of that day, their firm adherence to principle, even to the sacrifice of property and life, and the virtue and wisdom of the people who chose as their leaders, and sent to their assemblies and congresses, the ablest and best men of their several communities. What happened at Lexington and Concord, and all along the road from Concord back to Charlestown in the month of April a hundred years ago, was not an act of aggression against the British crown, but an act of defence of the constitutional rights symbolized by that crown, and of rights which were thereafter embodied in the written laws of the United States. Concord and Lexington were the best logical results of the long resistance of Boston and Massachusetts to "general warrants," to taxes laid without the consent of the colonists, to the invasion of the rights of property and the sanctity of the domicile, and to the many other usurpations of a parliament in which the colonies had no representation, accompanied as these infringements of natural and constitutional rights were accompanied by an obstinate purpose on the part of the advisers of the British crown, to establish them as law in the colonies by armed force. Thus were matters of vital principle upheld by the men of that day; and this is one of the lessons to be revived by the coming celebration. Another is, that the American people of 1775 and 1776, and for a generation following, had the virtue to choose for their representatives the men who best understood those principles, who would most conscientiously adhere to them, and to whom they could most safely intrust their highest interests. The review of the past, which the centennial celebration of Concord and Lexington will bring to us all, may also bring with it renewed and strengthened fidelity to the principles and virtues of our fathers. This, too, let us hope, will be among the best fruits of the centennial commemoration of that greatest political event in the history of mankind, which followed on the Fourth of July in the year succeeding Lexington and Concord, to the promotion and acceleration of which event the illustrious men of those neighborhoods devoted their fortunes and their lives, conspicuous amongst whom were, as I believe, your own immediate ancestors, as well as Warren and Revere and Dawes and the Adamses and Hancock.

Again thanking you for the privilege of accepting the invitation of the inhabitants of the town of Concord to unite with them in celebrating the centennial of so memorable an event,

I am very truly your obedient servant,

GEO. W. CHILDS.

HON. E. R. HOAR, R. W. EMERSON, ESQ., GEO. HEYWOOD, ESQ.,
Committee.

CHICOPEE, MASS., April 12, 1875.

GENTLEMEN, — I am in receipt of the kind invitation extended to me by the citizens of Concord, Mass., to be present as their guest, and to join with them in celebrating the centennial anniversary on the 19th inst., for which I desire to extend my sincere thanks.

I had hoped that my business engagements would admit of my accepting the invitation, but find it is not practicable.

I congratulate your committee in having secured in the "Minute Man," so fine a work of art in commemoration of the first who fell in the Revolutionary War. It is unquestionably the finest single statue ever erected in our Commonwealth. Yours very truly,

A. C. WOODWORTH,
Agent Ames Manufacturing Co.

HON. E. R. HOAR, R. W. EMERSON, GEO. HEYWOOD.

FLORENCE, ITALY, March 6, 1875.

GENTLEMEN, — Although my studies in Florence will render it impossible for me to be present at the celebration of the 19th of April, I would thank you most sincerely for the compliment you have shown me through your invitation.

To the town which I am proud to call my home, I must ever feel most deeply indebted; and I would express my grateful sense of the honor conferred on so inexperienced a man, by the confidence implied in the commission for a statue which is to commemorate so important an event.

If, by persevering in my profession, I am ever enabled to accomplish any thing worthy of my citizenship, I shall owe my gratitude to my friends at home for the encouragement they have so early and generously extended to me.

Thanking you again for your courteous remembrance of me,

I am, gentlemen, most respectfully and obediently,

DANIEL C. FRENCH.

HON. E. R. HOAR, R. W. EMERSON, GEO. HEYWOOD,
Committee of Invitation.

THE BALL.

THE BALL.

MANY of our guests remained to join in the festivities of the evening. Those who were present will appreciate our feeling, that no mere words can adequately portray the decorations, the dresses, the music, the enthusiasm, that made the grand ball so marked a success; but the account of Concord's great centennial celebration would be deemed to be incomplete, if it did not contain at least an attempt to preserve some of the bright colors of that happy occasion.

The following gentlemen composed the Ball Committee: —

Andrew J. Harlow, Henry J. Walcott, H. H. Buttrick, Richard F. Barrett, Sidney J. Barrett, James D. Wright, Samuel W. Brown, Samuel Hoar, Charles D. Tuttle, Joseph D. Brown, George P. How, James B. Wood.

Andrew J. Harlow was chosen manager, with

Henry J. Walcott, Henry J. Hosmer, George P. How, James C. Melvin, Joseph D. Brown, Richard F. Barrett, Samuel Hoar, and William Wheeler, as assistants, and

George M. Brooks, Richard Barrett, George Heywood, Reuben N. Rice, John S. Keyes, William W. Wilde, and George Keyes, to act as reception committee.

The Middlesex Agricultural Society generously permitted the committee to use their hall, situated on the Fair Grounds, on the bank of the Sudbury River, west of the Fitchburg Railroad Station. This building has an upper and lower hall, and several ante-rooms, which were heated for the occasion by a furnace, and lighted by gas.

The lower hall, used by the society for its annual exhibition of fruits and flowers, was decorated with great skill by Messrs. Lamprell and Marble of Boston. The entrance was through an arch, on the face of which was inscribed, "1775, April 19th, 1875;" and on each side were festoons of bunting, and flags of all nations, interspersed with shields. The hall, which is not finished or plastered, was thereby better fitted for the art of the decorator, who had so transformed it, that it was fairly ablaze with color. The ceiling was completely hidden by large flags, mostly those of the republics of the world, appropriately contrasted. The walls were curtained with festoons and drapery of flags of all nations, with naval signals and bunting. At intervals were placed trophies of sabre-blades, arranged in the form of stars, on a blue ground; also shields, representing the various seasons, and glories of American flags on staves tipped with gold. The floor was carpeted with white drilling, the effect of which more than counteracted the light-absorbing quality of the bunting.

The pillars through the centre of the hall were wreathed and draped with trophies of flags, and festoons and rosettes of bunting. Long streamers were stretched from pillar to pillar, and ribbons of red, white and blue bunting were looped and festooned along the cornices. Muskets, cutlasses, swords, pistols, and bayonets, were grouped on the pillars, or hung against the walls, in the forms of stars, shields, and sunbursts, and by their brilliancy relieved the almost monotonous beauty of the flags.

At each end of the hall was placed a platform for the musicians; and perhaps the most noticeable feature of the decorations was at the westerly end, the head of the hall, behind the grand orchestra. This was a device representing a globe resting on the shield of the United States, surmounted by an eagle holding in his beak a wreath of laurel and olive, and flanked on each side by American flags, and sun-bursts of muskets on a blue ground spangled with stars. A fragrant bank of hothouse-plants in full flower, massed together, concealed the platform from the floor to its edge.

From eight until after ten o'clock, select music was furnished for the promenade concert by the United States Marine Band of Washington, dressed in their showy uniforms of scarlet, assisted by the Grand Orchestra, under the direction of D. W. Reeves of Providence.

Dancing began at half-past ten o'clock, and continued until sunrise.

Prompted by the spirit of the occasion, many of the ladies wore the costumes of the last century. Family chests were ransacked, and the long-disused dresses of great-grandmothers were brought out. Rich brocades, long trains, puffed petticoats, torturing high-heeled slippers, powdered hair drawn up over cushions, high ruffs, with now and then a black patch, to add, by contrast, to the effect of a beautiful complexion, were conspicuous among the dancers, and presented a mass of rich, soft color, in strong and agreeable contrast to the prevailing hues of the decorations. The gentlemen, for the most part, wore the solemn black of the modern evening costume, but there were not wanting uniforms of the army and navy to add to the variety and brilliancy of the picture.

Altogether, the scene was one long to be remembered with pride and satisfaction, a fitting termination of so glorious a celebration. From half-past eleven until one o'clock, supper was served in the upper hall by William Tufts of Boston, in his most approved manner. This, the dining-hall of the society, was also decorated with bunting, and lighted with gas, and easily accommodated at its tables the large number of guests.

The charms of the music, and the fascination of dancing, triumphed over the fatigues attending so vast a celebration, and prolonged the ball, until, as the last dancers went homeward, they saw the sun rising.

So ended the celebration, twenty-four hours after the booming of cannon had announced its beginning.

THE LITERATURE
OF
THE NINETEENTH OF APRIL.

> And underneath is written,
>   In letters all of gold,
> How valiantly *they* kept the bridge
>   In the brave days of old.
>   *Lays of Ancient Rome.*

betw. 1 & 2 o'Clock

19 This Morng. we w.r alarm'd by y.e ring of y.e Bell — & upon Examn. fou.d y.t y.e Troops, to y.e N.o of 800, had stole y.r March from Boston in Boats & Barg.s from y.e Bottom of y.e Common over to a Point in Cambridge, near to Inman's Farm, & were at Lexington Meeting House, half an Hour before Sunrise, where they had fired upon a Body of our Men, & (as we after.ds heard) had killed several. This Intelligence was bro't us at 3.h by D.r Sam.ll Prescott who narrowly escap'd y.e Guard y.t were sent before on Horses, purposely to prevent all Posts & Messengers from giving us timely Information; He, by y.e Help of a very fleet Horse crossing several Walls and Fences, arriv'd at Concord at y.e Time abovemen.d When several Posts w.r immed dispatch'd that return confirm'd y.e Account of y.e Regulars Arrival at Lexington, & that they were on their Way to Concord. Upon this ac.t of our Minute Men belong.g to y.e Town, & Acton & Lincoln, with several others, y.t were in Readiness, march'd out to meet them, While y.e alarm Company w.r preparing to receive them in y.e Town. —
Capt. Minot who command.d y.e tho.t it proper to take Possess.n of y.e Hill above y.e meeting house as y.e most advantageous. No sooner had I gain'd than we were met by y.e Companies y.t were

sent out to meet ye Troops, who inform'd us, yt were just upon us, & that we must retreat, as their No. was more than threeble to ours.— We then retreat'd for ye Hill near Liberty Pole & took a new Post back of ye Town, upon a rising Eminence, were we form'd into two Battalions & waited ye Arrival of ye Enemy. Scarcely had we form'd, before we saw ye brittish Troops, at ye Distan of a ¼ of a Mile, glittering in Arms, advancing to- wards with ye greatest Celerity. Some were for making a Stand, notw'g ye Super' of ye No. but others more prudent tho't best to retreat till our Strenth shd be equal to ye Enemy's by Recruits from neigh'g Towns yt were contin' coms' on to our Assistance. Accordingly we retreat'd. over ye Bridge, when ye Troops came into ye Town, — set fire to seve- ral Carriages for ye Artillery, destroy'd 60 Barrels of flour, rifled sev Houses. — took Possession of ye Town house, destroy'd 500lb of Ball set a Guard of 100 Men at ye N Bridge, & S Sent up a Party to ye Hou of Col. Barrett, were they were in Expecta of finding a Quan of War -like Stores; but these were happily secur'd just before their Arrival, by Transpor into ye Woods & othr by-Places. — In ye mean Time, the Guard set by ye Enemy to secure ye Pass at ye N. Bridge, were alarm by ye Approa of our People, who had retreated as men before, & wr. now advancing, with Str'ee Ord'rs not to

not to fire upon ye Troops, unless fir'd upon — These Orders were so punctually observ'd yt. we rec'd ye Fire of ye Enemy in 3 several & seperate Discharges of their Pieces, before it was return'd, by our command Officer; the firing then soon becā general for few min:s in wch Skirmish two W:re kill'd on each Side, & few of ye Enemy wounded: — It may here be obs:d by ye Way, if we were ye more can be prevent begin a Rupture wth ye K's Troops, as we w:re then uncert:n what had happ: at Lexington, & knew if they had began ye Quarrell there by ye. firing upon our ppl & killing 8 Men upon ye List. — The Troops soon quitted their Post at ye Bridge, & retreat:d in gt Disord:r & haste to ye main Body, who were soon upon ye March to meet them. — For half an hour ye Enemy by ye Marches & counter Marches discover'd a Fickleness & Inconstancy of Mind, sometimes advancing sometimes returning to ye former Posts, till at length they quitted ye Town, & retreated by ye Way yy came. thō in ye Mean Time, a Party of our Men (150) took ye back Way thro' of ye Fields, into ye Eg:r & had plac'd 'em to advantage, laying in Ambush, behind Walls fences & Buildings, & to fire upon ye Enemy, on their Retreat

THE NINETEENTH OF APRIL IN LITERATURE.

[PREPARED BY JAMES L. WHITNEY[1].]

This Month remar[kable] for ye g^{test} Events taking Pla[ce] in ye pr[esent] Age.
Entry in the Diary of the Reverend William Emerson, April, 1775.

1775.

THE materials for a full and exact history of the events of this time can be found neither in contemporary public documents nor in the popular accounts of the day.

The official records of the Second Provincial Congress, which met at Cambridge, Concord, and Watertown, from February 1 to May 29, have, in great part, been lost. This is owing, it is thought, to the confusion arising from the changes of the place of meeting, and from the suddenness of the march of the British force to Concord. Documents of importance may have been purposely destroyed, lest they should fall into the hands of the enemy. We are not, however, without much of an authentic character. This can be found in a work prepared by William Lincoln, and published by the State of Massachusetts in 1838. The Journals of the First, Second, and Third Provincial Congress, are here reprinted, together with the Journals of the Committee of Safety and of the Committee of Supplies. The last include the record of several meetings at Concord in April, with the addresses to the people of Massachusetts and other colonies.

This publication contains also the following:—

The list of the Provincials killed, wounded, and missing on the Nineteenth of April.

The Circumstantial Account sent by General Gage to Governor Trumbull of Connecticut.

The Report of the Committee on the damages done on the line of march of the king's troops, and copies of letters written after the attack.

The student of the history of this time will find Force's "American Archives" an important source of information, the statements of which should, however, be confirmed by other authorities. This is a documentary

---

[1] Acknowledgment is due to Mr. Justin Winsor for the use made of his article on Centennial Reading in the Bulletin of the Boston Public Library.

history of the colonies to 1787, and contains, besides various documents already mentioned, the following:—

The Instructions of General Gage to Captain Brown and Ensign De Berniere[1] [De Bernière,?] February 22, 1775, ordering sketches to be made of the country between Boston and Worcester, with the Narrative of De Berniere; also, various political pamphlets which appeared in America and Great Britain at this time; the proceedings of Parliament, and of various legislative bodies in America; extracts from public and private letters; an account of the events which followed the Nineteenth of April; the proceedings of the conventions of the people in the counties of Massachusetts; and narratives of the excursion and ravages of the king's troops, with the depositions taken by order of the Provincial Congress; also, the following:—

"An account of the commencement of Hostilities between Great Britain and America, in the Province of the Massachusetts-Bay. By the Reverend Mr. William Gordon of Roxbury, in a Letter to a Gentleman in England, dated May 17, 1775;" with other papers.

Almon's "Remembrancer" was established about this time at London, with a view of gathering together important political papers, American and British. To this collection all writers upon the American Revolution have been largely indebted. Almon was hostile to the ministerial party, and his collection, therefore, includes mostly letters, speeches, and publications that favor the interests of the colonists.

Accounts of the events of the Nineteenth of April appeared first in newspapers and broadsides. According to Thomas's "History of Printing," in April, 1775, there were five newspapers published in Boston. Of these, two were removed,—"The Massachusetts Spy" to Worcester, just before the nineteenth, and "The Boston Gazette" to Watertown. Two others suspended publication. There were, besides these, only two newspapers in Massachusetts, and nine in New England. In New York there were four (or, as it is now believed, only three), and in the British colonies, now comprised in the United States, thirty-seven.

"The Massachusetts Spy" published the report of the events of the day in its first issue at Worcester, May 3. The accounts in the "Essex Gazette," and in "The Salem Gazette, or Newbury and Marblehead Advertiser," appeared in the numbers for April 21, 25, and May 5. These last, with a list of the killed and wounded, and a funeral elegy, were published at Salem, 1775, in a handbill, entitled "Bloody Butchery, by the British Troops; or the Runaway Fight of the Regulars. Being the Particulars of the Victorious Battle fought at and near Concord, situated Twenty Miles from Boston, in the Province of the Massachusetts-Bay, between Two Thousand Regular Troops, belonging to His Britannic Majesty, and a few Hundred Provincial Troops, belonging to the

---

[1] Called, probably incorrectly, by some authorities, Bernicre. Henry De Berniere made a plan of the battle of Bunker Hill, which was engraved and published in "The Analectic Magazine," February, 1818, and which is said to be the first plan that appeared in an American engraving. It is there represented to be from a sketch found in the captured baggage of a British officer in 1775.

Province of Massachusetts-Bay, which lasted from sunrise until sunset, on the 19th of April, 1775, when it was decided greatly in favor of the latter." Above the title were forty coffins, on which were the names of the Americans who were then reported to be killed.

The Narrative of the Reverend William Emerson, who was a spectator of the action at the North Bridge, is in the form of a diary, written upon blank leaves inserted in an almanac, and is dated April 19, 1775. This was first printed in R. W. Emerson's "Historical Discourse," 1835, at the second centennial anniversary of the incorporation of the town of Concord. This pamphlet was republished in 1875. A heliotype of the original manuscript (now in the possession of R. W. Emerson, a grandson of the author) is given at the beginning of this article.[1]

During the week after the battle, the depositions of citizens of Concord and Lexington were taken by order of the Provincial Congress, and a narrative was prepared by a committee. These were printed in American and English newspapers, and were sent to the Continental Congress, to every town in the province, and to Great Britain. They were published subsequently by Isaiah Thomas, by order of the Provincial Congress, in a pamphlet, with the title "Narrative of the Excursion and Ravages of the King's Troops under the Command of Gen. Gage, on the Nineteenth of April, 1775. Together with the Depositions taken by order of Congress to support the Truth of it." These important documents have been frequently reprinted. Most of the original manuscripts are in the Library of Harvard College, where also can be found manuscript letters of Joseph Warren, Cambridge, April 27 and May 16, and John Dickinson, April 29, 1775, all touching upon the events of the Nineteenth of April.

The letters and journals, which were written at this time, add much to our knowledge of events. They are too numerous to be mentioned in detail. The following have been published by the Massachusetts Historical Society:

A Letter from Colonel Paul Revere to the Corresponding Secretary of the Society. This is dated January 1, 1798, and gives an account of his memorable ride.[2]

A Journal kept during the Time y^t Boston was shut up in 1775-6. By Timothy Newell, Esqr., one of the Select Men of the Town. This begins April 19.[3]

Letters of John Andrews, Esq., of Boston, 1772-1776. Compiled and edited from the original MSS. by Winthrop Sargent.[4]

Letters of David Greene and Joseph Greene, Boston, May 6 and 10, 1775.[5]

Letter of Doctor Isaac Foster (?), April 18, 21, 1775.[6]

---

[1] Mr. Emerson states in his Historical Discourse that the context and the testimony of some of the surviving veterans incline him to think that the word *not* was accidentally omitted [before the last word (yt) in the tenth line from the top of the third column of this manuscript].

[2] Collections, Series I., vol. 5.
[3] Collections, Series IV., vol 1.
[4] Proceedings, July, 1865.
[5] Proceedings, June, 1873.
[6] Proceedings, April, 1870.

Papers in regard to the carrying of the news of the battle to England.[1] Also other documents already mentioned.

The manuscript Diary of the Reverend Ezra Stiles of Newport, afterwards president of Yale College, contains particulars of the events of this and of the subsequent time. It gives a relation of Major Pitcairn's version of the beginning of the firing. This Diary is in the Library of Yale College.

Letters can be found, also, in Niles's "Principles and Acts of the Revolution," in "The Detail and Conduct of the American War," published before 1780, in Dawson's "Historical Magazine," and in the general collections mentioned at the beginning of this article.

"The Journal of the Continental Congress," and "The Parliamentary Register," contain the proceedings of these bodies at this time. "The Parliamentary History of England," and the "Journals of the House of Lords" and the "Journals of the House of Commons," should also be consulted.

English accounts of the battle, and of its effects upon the nation, with discussions of its political bearings, can be found in the English papers of the time, and in "The Annual Register" for 1775. In this work, the articles upon the American Revolution were written principally, if not wholly, by Edmund Burke.

Lord Mahon (Earl Stanhope) appends to the account of the battle, in his "History of England," the official report of Lieutenant-Colonel Smith to General Gage, also a letter from Edward Gibbon the historian, dated May 31, 1775.

John Horne, who was afterwards called Horne Tooke, and became celebrated as the author of "The Diversions of Purley," was brought to trial in 1777, before the King's Bench. He was charged with libelling the king in publishing the statement that the Americans were inhumanly murdered by the king's troops at Lexington and Concord. He was condemned to imprisonment for twelve months, and to pay a fine of two hundred pounds. The case is reported at length, and is interesting as showing the state of feeling in England.[2]

Accounts of the Nineteenth of April were published, in 1776, in Lowe's and in George's Almanacs; also in Stearns's North American Almanac. The first two were written by the Reverend William Gordon of Roxbury, who made use of the material in his "History of the Rise, Progress, and Establishment of the Independence of the United States of America. London, 1788."

A pamphlet was published at Boston, in 1779, containing General Gage's Instructions, and De Berniere's Report, with an Account of the Transactions of the British Troops, and a List of their killed, wounded, and missing.

At Lexington, on the first anniversary, the Reverend Jonas Clark delivered a sermon, which was published in 1776, and reprinted in 1875. The day was

---

[1] Proceedings, April, 1858.
[2] Rex vs. Horne. Cowper, 672. — Howell's State Trials. xx. 651-802.

celebrated in this town for eight successive years, 1776-1783, and the anniversary sermons were printed. They can be found in the Library of the Massachusetts Historical Society.

The "Brief Narrative of the Principal Transactions of that Day," which was appended to Clark's sermon, was republished in 1875, in folio, with heliotypes of four engravings, which were published at New Haven in 1775. Of the pictorial representations which appeared at this time, these are especially worthy of mention. They are described as "neatly engraven on copper from original paintings taken on the spot." The artists, Earl, a portrait-painter, and Amos Doolittle, an engraver, were soldiers in the New Haven company that set out for Cambridge, April 20. One of the plates gives a view of Concord, with the ministerial troops destroying the stores; another (given in reduced size in this volume), the battle at the North Bridge. There are views also of the attack at Lexington and of the retreat of the British troops. The original plates were twelve by eighteen inches in size.

There is a view of Concord in 1776, in "The Massachusetts Magazine," July, 1794.

John Boyle's "Eulogium on Major-General Joseph Warren, by a Columbian," Boston, 1781, contains a poetical description of the battle. Samuel Langdon, President of Harvard College, in a sermon preached before the Provincial Congress at Watertown, May 31, 1775, alludes to the events of the preceding month. This sermon was published in 1775, and republished in J. Wingate Thornton's "Pulpit of the American Revolution."

1800.

The preceding works include most of the contemporary publications which have come down to us. From 1800 until 1825, but little appeared, except in general histories and in biographies. Among these are Mrs. Mercy Warren's "History of the Rise, Progress and Termination of the American Revolution" (1805), James Thacher's "Military Journal during the American Revolutionary War" (1823), and the "Memoirs of Major-General Heath" (1798), who, late in the day, acted as commander of the Provincials.

1825.

In 1825, the semi-centennial anniversary was celebrated at Concord, Edward Everett delivering the oration, which was published the same year. Accounts of the proceedings are given in "The Concord Gazette and Middlesex Yeoman," and in other newspapers. The same year, Elias Phinney's "History of the Battle at Lexington" was published, followed, in 1827, by the Reverend Doctor Ezra Ripley's "History of the Fight at Concord . . . showing that then and there the first regular and forcible Resistance was made to the British Soldiery, and the first British Blood was shed by armed Americans, and the Revolutionary War thus commenced." The title indicates the points in controversy between these authors and the two towns. These were, whether the British fire was first returned at Lexington, or at Concord. Ripley's book was republished in 1832, and Phinney's in 1875. It was claimed that neither account gave due credit to Captain Davis and his men; and, in 1835 and 1850, Josiah Adams, in an address and in a letter, detailed the honorable part Acton had taken in the events of the day. In a pamphlet of six pages, published about 1835, **Rufus Hosmer** of Stow reviews the first three of the above. The three works by Phinney, Ripley, and Adams, contain depositions made at the time of their preparation by survivors of the fight. Happily the echo of this controversy had quite died away before the coming of the centennial year.

In 1835, Shattuck's "History of Concord" was published, containing a detailed account of the history of the town in 1775, and during the Revolution. This work, which has become quite rare, is regarded as an accurate, and important contribution to the early history of New England.

Lexington celebrated the sixtieth anniversary in 1835. Edward Everett delivered the oration, which was published in a pamphlet containing an account of the proceedings. It was republished in 1875. This oration, and that at Concord ten years before, can be found in the first volume of Everett's "Orations and Speeches."

The same year, Danvers laid the corner-stone of a monument in memory of the seven citizens of the town who were killed on the Nineteenth of April. Daniel P. King delivered an address, which was published.

1850.

On the seventy-fifth anniversary, there was a union celebration at Concord, by the towns of Concord, Lexington, Acton, Lincoln, Sudbury, Bedford, and Carlisle. The oration, by Robert Rantoul, junior, was published the same year, with an Appendix containing an account of the proceedings on the occasion. The Concord Free Public Library has preserved in a scrap-book, prepared by William W. Wheildon, newspaper cuttings giving the order of exercises, the oration, the after-dinner speeches by Everett, Choate, Palfrey, and others; also, in manuscript, the minutes of the meetings of the committee, as well as the letters received from the invited guests.

The parts taken by Acton, West Cambridge, Cambridge, and Lexington, have also been commemorated by public celebrations, in 1851, 1864, 1870, and 1871. The addresses, by George S. Boutwell, Samuel A. Smith, the Reverend Alexander McKenzie, and George B. Loring, have been published. John Pierpont was the author of the poem at the first-mentioned celebration. It is not contained in any edition of his works.

In 1851 there was published, in a pamphlet of forty-six pages, by request of the town of Acton, the Speech delivered in the House of Representatives of Massachusetts, February 3, 1851, by James Trask Woodbury, upon the question of granting two thousand dollars to aid the town in building a monument over the remains of Captain Isaac Davis, Abner Hosmer, and James Hayward.

In 1852, Josiah Adams published, in a pamphlet of eight pages, a "Letter to the people of Acton, relative to the evidence which procured the grant for the Davis monument."

One of the chapters in Edward Everett's "Mount Vernon Papers," published in 1860, is entitled "The Nineteenth of April, 1775."

"Concord Fight," a poem by S. R. Bartlett, and "The Fight at Lexington," an illustrated ballad by Thomas D. English, appeared in 1860, the latter in "Harper's New Monthly Magazine." Charles Hudson's "History of Lexington" was published in 1868. More than one hundred pages of this work are devoted to the events of the Nineteenth of April.

1875.

In regard to the Centennial Celebration, but little need be added to the record given in the preceding pages. An address was delivered March 30, before the people of Concord, by the Reverend Grindall Reynolds. This appeared later in "The Unitarian Review and Religious Magazine," and as an independent pamphlet. An illustrated article by Frederic Hudson, entitled "The Concord Fight," was published in "Harper's New Monthly Magazine," in May. The Ode at the Concord Centennial, by James Russell Lowell, was first published in "The Atlantic Monthly," June, 1875.

"Potter's American Monthly," April, 1875, contains an account of Jonathan Harrington, the last survivor of the fight.

The proceedings at Lexington were published by order of the town. The oration, by Richard H. Dana, junior, has been separately printed.

The Reverend Henry Westcott delivered, April 11, 18, and 25, three sermons in the First Congregational Church at Lexington. They were published as "Lexington Centennial Sermons" the same year.

"The New-England Historical and Genealogical Register," October, 1875, contains the orations and accounts of the proceedings at Concord and Lexington.

The Reports for 1875–1876 of the town officers of Concord and Lexington give further particulars in regard to the two celebrations.

At the time of the Centennial Celebration, statements hitherto unpublished related the part taken in the fight by Jonas Brown[1] and Amos Barrett,[2] both of Concord. The former, although wounded at the North Bridge, joined in the pursuit of the enemy through the day. He enlisted afterwards to serve through the war, and became a lieutenant.

The enterprise of the present day is strikingly contrasted with the past in the publicity given by the press to this celebration; the Semi-Centennial having received only the notice of a paragraph in most of the Boston papers.

---

[1] Lowell Courier.   [2] Cincinnati Times.

Of the innumerable publications issued at this time, — pamphlets, magazines, newspapers, circulars, photographs, and engravings, — much has been collected by the Public Libraries of Concord and Boston, where, also, are to be preserved the original manuscripts of the orations, poems, and correspondence.

GENERAL WORKS.

The authorities thus far mentioned are confined mainly to the Nineteenth of April, and to the events immediately preceding and following. Other more comprehensive works, show the connection of the events of this day with the history of the times. Of these, Frothingham's "History of the Siege of Boston, and of the Battles of Lexington, Concord, and Bunker Hill," is first to be mentioned for its thoroughness.

The Histories of the United States, by Hildreth and by Bancroft, "The History of Massachusetts," by Barry, and Dawson's "Battles of the United States by Sea and Land," contain chapters upon this period. Edward E. Hale's "One Hundred Years Ago" is a fresh presentation of the subject. Other authorities do not need mention here.

Of early English authorities, Adolphus and Belsham are best known. The former defends the British ministry; the latter, the Americans. "The History of the Origin, Progress, and Termination of the American War," by C. Stedman (1794), details military operations. The author criticises the movements of Howe, Clinton, and Cornwallis, under whom he served. Andrews's History (1785) should also be consulted, and Aikin's "Annals of the Reign of King George the Third" (1816). Among later authorities are Hughes's "History of England" (1835), Smyth's chapters on the American Revolution in his "Lectures on Modern History" (1839), Stanhope (already mentioned), and Massey's "History of England during the Reign of George the Third" (1858).

The Oxford Prize Essay, 1869, by John Andrew Doyle, on "The American Colonies previous to the Declaration of Independence" deserves especial mention in this place. It is admirable in its spirit, and masterly in its treatment.

The part taken in the fight at Concord and Lexington by the British regiments is mentioned in the historical records of those regiments, which have been published by the War Department.

The lives of the leaders in the opening scenes of the Revolution present vivid pictures of the times. Such are the biographies of Franklin and Washington, of the Adamses and Hancock, of Warren, Putnam, Gerry, and Timothy Pickering.

The last mentioned has been blamed for not appearing upon the scene of action with the Essex regiment, on the Nineteenth of April. He is defended by Swett, in a pamphlet entitled, "Defence of Pickering against Bancroft," and also in "The Life of Timothy Pickering," by his son, Octavius Pickering.

The various biographies of George the Third are important sources of information for the student of this period, as well as the speeches and correspondence of Burke, Lord Chatham, Fox, and Lord North.

The views of the best French and German authorities can be found in the following : —

Chas and Lebrun. "Histoire politique et philosophique de la Révolution de l'Amérique septentrionale. Paris, 1800."

É. R. L. Laboulaye. "Histoire politique des États-Unis ... 1620–1789. Paris, 1855–1866."

M. C. Sprengel. "Geschichte der Revolution in Amerika. Speier, 1785."

K. F. Neumann. "Geschichte der Vereinigten Staaten von Amerika. Berlin, 1863–1866."

Of the poetry and fiction called forth by the events of the Nineteenth of April, the most important are Longfellow's "Paul Revere's Ride," Hawthorne's "Septimius Felton," and the familiar Hymn by Ralph Waldo Emerson. To these should be added the poems by John G. Whittier, and Oliver Wendell Holmes.

The verses on the "Story of the Battle at Concord," etc., by "Eb. Stiles," written March 15, 1795, of which the manuscript is in the Library of the Massachusetts Historical Society, deserve mention only on account of their age and patriotic fervor.

In Cooper's "Lionel Lincoln," a tale of the American Revolution, two chapters describe the advance of the British to Concord, and their retreat. This story has been dramatized by Stephen E. Glover, in "The Cradle of Liberty, or Boston in 1775."

Hawthorne makes the adventures of the "Grandfather's Chair," which passed from one distinguished man to another for nearly two centuries, tell the story of the Nineteenth of April as a part of its account of the early history of this country.

As this volume goes to press, a centennial drama, by Doctor J. S. Jones, is being represented at the Boston Museum. It is entitled "Paul Revere and the Sons of Liberty," and its scenes include the battles at Concord, Lexington, Bunker Hill, and the siege and evacuation of Boston.

APPENDIX.

(A.)

LEXINGTON, Nov. 12, 1873.

GENTLEMEN, — The cherished desire of the citizens of Lexington to celebrate the one hundredth anniversary of the 19th of April, 1775, assumed a tangible form at our annual meeting on the 4th inst., when the undersigned were chosen a committee, "to take such preliminary steps as they may deem expedient, towards preparing for a centennial celebration of the 19th of April, 1775." We communicate this to you to solicit your good services in awakening a popular interest among the people of your town; so that, before any specific arrangements are made, you may be enabled to participate with us in commemoration of an event in which we have a common interest, and which has made *Concord* and *Lexington* household words, not only in this country, but in Europe. Being thus connected, we trust you will unite with us as cordially as we united with you in celebrating the seventy-fifth anniversary.

We hope to have a celebration worthy of the day, when we shall be able to unveil the statues of the proscribed patriots Hancock and Adams; so that the statesman and the soldier may stand forth together in our Memorial Hall as equally worthy of our veneration and gratitude.

In due time you may expect a more direct and full invitation to join us in commemorating the valor and disinterested patriotism displayed by our fathers over the whole field, from Concord North Bridge to Charlestown Neck.

We are, gentlemen, very respectfully,

Your humble servants,

CHARLES HUDSON,
M. H. MERRIAM,   } *Committee.*
R. W. REED,

TO THE HON. BOARD OF SELECTMEN OF CONCORD, MASS.

(B.)

CONCORD, Jan. 12, 1874.

GENTLEMEN, — Your communication of the 12th November last, extending an invitation to the town of Concord to unite with you in celebrating the one hundredth anniversary of the 19th of April, 1775, was duly received, and we owe you an apology for not replying earlier; but we have delayed doing so, thinking we might have a town meeting, at which we could bring the matter before the town. The subject of a celebration on that day has been talked of among some of our prominent men for several months. The town of Concord, as you are aware, celebrated the fiftieth and the seventy-fifth anniversary of the day, and had proposed to have a good *centennial* celebration, at which time we propose to dedicate a statue of a continental minute-man, to be erected at the battle-ground. A committee was chosen at the annual meeting in March, 1873, to procure a model of a statue, which was accepted at the November meeting, and the work is now in course of construction. In view of the action of the town before receiving your communication, and knowing the desire of our citizens to celebrate the day in a proper manner, we feel that it would be exceeding our authority to speak definitely in relation to your invitation, without laying the subject before the town, which we will do at our annual meeting in March, with the view of having a committee appointed to confer with you in relation to a joint observance of the day, in which we certainly have a common interest.

Very respectfully yours,

HENRY F. SMITH,
WILLIAM W. WILDE, } *Selectmen of Concord.*
JOHN B. MOORE,

HON. CHARLES HUDSON, M. H. MERRIAM, R. W. REED,

Committee, Lexington.

www.ingramcontent.com/pod-product-compliance
Lightning Source LLC
Chambersburg PA
CBHW020246170426
43202CB00008B/251